Front and back cover photos by Tom Smarch Photography
Pictured on front from left to right:

Paul Moon, Kimberly Warbington Parris, Paula Delgado, Stephen Harris, Ken Almon, Jonathan Harris, Kimberly Foster, Alan Michaels, Mark Little, Amit Momaya

Paul Moon

Paul was a member of my 1988–1989 fifth-grade class. He is now a special education teacher at Sandy Creek High School in Fayette County, Georgia.

Kimberly Warbington Parris

I taught Kim in 1984 during my first year as a teacher. Kim is a mother of four and has maintained contact with me since she finished fifth grade.

Paula Delgado

Paula was a member of my 2002–2003 fifth-grade class. She currently attends Summerour Middle School where she is serving her second year as student council president. Paula serves as a mentor to my current classes and speaks frequently at our academic honor celebrations. She is an incredibly talented person and is on the road to greatness.

Stephen Harris

Stephen was in my fifth-grade class in 1991–1992. He won a track scholarship to the University of Tennessee, where he was a four-time all-American and the 2003 NCAA decathlon champion. He competed in the 2004 U.S. Olympic trials and continues to hold fast to his dream of making the 2008 U.S. Olympic Team. Stephen was recently hired to teach eighth grade social studies and coach cross country and track and field at Cleveland Middle School in Cleveland, Tennessee.

Jonathan Harris

Jonathan was one of my 1990–1991 fifth-grade students and is the older brother of Stephen. He recently partnered with friends to open a computer technology company called Commercial Net, where he currently serves as vice president of technology.

Kimberly Foster

Kim was a member of my fifth-grade class in 1991–1992. She is currently a language arts teacher at Osborne Middle School in Gwinnett County, Georgia. Kim was born to be a teacher.

Alan Michaels

Alan was a student in my 1990–1991 fifth-grade class. Throughout his high school years, Alan organized tutoring groups to work with Norcross Elementary students. Alan attended Georgia Tech and is now a systems engineer.

Mark Little

Mark was a member of my 1985–1986 fifth-grade class. He is currently a Fulton County deputy marshal and the father of a little girl.

Amit Momaya

Amit was a fifth-grade student of mine during the 1995–1996 school year. Amit graduated as salutatorian from Norcross High School and is currently studying medicine at Duke University.

Finding Favor with Your Students

Finding Favor with Your Students

✦

National Award-Winning Educator Shares Strategies on Becoming the Teacher Your Students Would Choose

Ken Almon

iUniverse, Inc.
New York Lincoln Shanghai

Finding Favor with Your Students
National Award-Winning Educator Shares Strategies on Becoming the Teacher Your Students Would Choose

iUniverse books may be ordered through booksellers or by contacting:

iUniverse
2021 Pine Lake Road, Suite 100
Lincoln, NE 68512
www.iuniverse.com
1-800-Authors (1-800-288-4677)

ISBN-13: 978-0-595-36480-0 (pbk)
ISBN-13: 978-0-595-80913-4 (ebk)
ISBN-10: 0-595-36480-2 (pbk)
ISBN-10: 0-595-80913-8 (ebk)

Printed in the United States of America

To Mom and Dad

Thanks for being wonderful parents and my real-life heroes.

To My Family

Thanks for supporting and loving me and helping me become the person I am today.

To My Colleagues

Thanks for being patient with me and allowing me to do my own thing but still feel part of the team.

To My Administrators

Thanks for always supporting me and allowing me to teach "out of the box" and do what I think is good for kids.

To All My Students

Thanks for giving me the honor of being a part of your lives.

You are forever a part of me as I am of you.

I continue to expect great things from you.

Do Good! Be Good! Do Good Work! Keep in Touch!

In Memory of

Don Jones

Devaughn "Fridge" Smith

Michael Btembke

Three students who went before their time…you will live forever in my heart.

Contents

Acknowledgments

Writing this book has prompted me to reflect on those who influenced my life in the past and those who continue to affect my life now.

Thanks, Dad, for being my hero. You have touched so many lives with your gracious, giving spirit. I know Mom would be proud to see me stepping into the classroom each day, following in both her footsteps and yours. Thanks, Mom, for instilling in me a love for reading and words. I still miss you dearly.

Thanks to my family for your love and support. Annie Grace, Althea, Robert, Denise, Frank, and Sheryl, I will always be your baby brother. Thanks also to my maternal and paternal aunts, uncles, and cousins. Thanks to Aunt Rozie Lewis for paving the way by being the first African American to graduate from college in Haralson County, the county of my birth. Thanks to Aunt Alvesta Springer for your example in demonstrating to us how to hold fast to dreams by obtaining your Early Childhood Education degree at the age of seventy and graduating with honors. What a blessing to have been born in such an amazing family! There's nothing so powerful as family.

Thanks to all the principals and teachers I have had the pleasure of working with over the past twenty-plus years: Cindy Antrim, Dr. Jan Hall, Gary Yetter, Jean Walker, Dr. Angela Pringle, and Dr. Lavern Watkins. I give a special thanks to Cindy Antrim, who took the risk of hiring a small-town boy from Tallapoosa, Georgia, and gave me a chance to teach. Special thanks to Eve Hunter, a true friend, who has supported me throughout my entire teaching career.

Thanks to Dr. Frances E. Davis, Dr. Mary Kay Murphy, and Mr. J. Alvin Wilbanks, superintendent of Gwinnett County Public Schools, for your leadership and support. Thanks also to the students of Norcross Elementary.

Thanks to Gary "Fish" Fischer, Helen Morris, and Sherry "Tammy" Bradford for encouraging me and helping me get my thoughts down in book form. I finally did it! Thank you, Crystal Marshall, for being such a good friend. You are an awesome teacher. Thank you, Julie Pugh, for always making me smile. Thanks, Gary Grimac, for being a good friend and colleague at the start of my career. Let's continue to share ideas, Guido. *Kensuke's Kingdom* was a great read!

Thanks to the staff and teachers of Norcross Elementary School. It is my pleasure to be able to work alongside such an incredible and hardworking staff. Continue to put children first. Thanks to Bonnie Daniels, Becky Barton, Peggy Usry, Susan Parker, Allen Brumbalow, and other longtime Norcross Elementary School teachers for your commitment to the students at Norcross Elementary. Thanks for choosing to stay.

Thanks to Valerie Anderson and your custodial staff for being so understanding of my teaching style—I know it makes my classroom very difficult to keep clean. Thanks also, Tom Smarch, for your assistance with the cover photographs. God bless you, brother.

Thanks to coach Randy Patterson for being like a big brother to me and being so actively involved in my life during my teen years. Thank you, coach Ralph Hilburn and Mr. Charles Calhoun, for your support doing my time at Haralson County High School.

Thanks to Herschel Kirkland and Randy Garrett for being my high school buddies. We will forever be the three amigos.

Thanks to Mike Hadaway and Bob Howard for your friendship. You were great college roommates. Always remember, *Life for me ain't been no crystal stair.*

Thanks to Dr. Paul Phillips, Dr. Lucy Klee, Dr. Faris, and Dr. Tom Davidson for so profoundly influencing my teaching philosophy during my years at the University of West Georgia. You are all remarkable. Thanks to campus ministers John Caylor and Bobby Evans, who guided me spiritually during my years at West Georgia.

Thanks to the Milken Family Foundation for selecting me to receive a national educator award and to Mayor Lillian Webb of Norcross for presenting me with a key to the city during my Milken Award reception.

Thanks to the Delgado family for accepting me as part of your family and permitting me to work on parts of this book at your kitchen table. I give a special thanks to Paula Delgado for keeping me company and writing alongside me during our joint writing sessions. Thanks for letting me continue to be a part of your life.

I give a final thanks to all the students I have had the honor of teaching over the past twenty years. You are the only reason I teach. You are forever a part of me, as I am of you. If this book ever crosses your path, please get in touch with me. I would love to hear from you. You may reach me by e-mail at ken_almon@gwinnett.k12.ga.us.

Introduction

Have you ever considered what would happen if students were allowed to choose their own teachers? Would your name be at the top of their list? Are students praying and dreaming they will be in your class, or would they consider life in your room a never-ending nightmare? Are all classrooms created equal?

I wrote *Finding Favor with Your Students: Becoming the Teacher Your Students Would Choose* to share what I've learned during my twenty years in the classroom. I began my career two decades ago after graduating from the University of West Georgia with a master's degree in middle grades education. I was hired to teach fifth grade at Norcross Elementary, in Norcross, Georgia, and I have taught there ever since. Like all teachers, I started out determined to make a difference in the lives of my students. I have always strived to provide my students with more than just the academic basics and to keep them motivated and excited about learning. My teaching philosophy is alive and always changing.

So what makes a teacher a child's favorite? What makes one classroom more exciting than another? In *Finding Favor with Your Students*, you won't find the latest research or theories on the best reading practices or any other academic subject. The purpose of this book is to highlight the personal side of teaching, the side that is often overlooked in today's high stress "test, test, test" climate. This book offers ideas and strategies that will help you as a teacher, whether you're a veteran educator or new to the profession, gain favor with the students you find in your classroom each year. You will read about techniques you can use to motivate your students and help them feel good about who they are and what they have to offer.

I measure the success of the strategies I discuss in this book not by a grading scale or score on a standardized test, but rather by the smiles on my students' faces and the dance in their eyes. I see these strategies at work in the way my students treat one another and the adults they see every day, and in their loyalty and the way they try to move mountains to please me.

Although I had excellent college professors, the majority of what you will read in *Finding Favor with Your Students* was not learned in a university classroom or a college textbook, but from colleagues and by trial and error on the front lines day after day, year after year.

The meaning of *favor* is *to find pleasure, desire, and delight.* It means to be pleased with someone and to show partiality. Too many teachers make the mistake of trying too hard to get their students to like them. I tell my students on the first day of school that getting them to like me is not my number one priority. The first part of each school year, I have to do a tremendous amount of training and chiseling, removing behaviors I know could interfere with the learning and direction I have planned for the class. One definition of training is *to twist into greatness.* At the beginning of each year, I place a lot of emphasis on little things, so they won't become major problems later in the year. This process of training, or twisting into greatness, is needed less and less as the year progresses.

I let my students know that contrary to popular opinion, what most students really want is a class where the teacher is in control and things are done in an orderly way. They want an environment conducive to learning. Taking control gains favor. The environment and atmosphere you set up, how you teach, and the strategies and activities you use will determine whether or not your students find *pleasure, desire, and delight* in you.

Since my first year in the classroom, I have had the pleasure of former students returning to see me and say thanks. As a new teacher, I thought this was common practice, but after a few years I found out how truly uncommon such visits are. Even after twenty years of visitations, I get deeply moved when former students, especially those who have grown into adults, take the time to drop by my classroom. It was through hearing from these former students that I began to understand the impact I had had on their lives. It was thanks to these visits, coupled with the letters and phone calls I received, that *Finding Favor with Your Students* was written.

I have often been asked to share my secrets to gain favor with students. That's what this book is for. As you will find out, there really are no secrets, but rather sensible, practical strategies that are easy to apply. Some of these strategies are short and to the point and require little or no elaboration. None are rigid, so feel free to adapt them to best meet your students' needs. Try out a few at a time—there's no need to incorporate everything at once.

I have found the strategies described in this book to be quite effective in getting and keeping students on my team. Keep in mind that I make no claim to be an expert or to know all the answers, only that I have found success with these practical strategies for team building and gaining favor with students. It is my hope that you too will gain the favor of the students you work with throughout your career.

Finding Favor with Your Students

1

Greet Your Students Each Day

One of the greatest needs human beings have is to be recognized. Students, no matter their age, are no different. They need to know they are valued and important.

I let my students know they are valued by greeting them each morning at the classroom door. At the beginning of the school year, my students are usually not accustomed to this, and sometimes try to walk past me into the room without responding to my greeting. I teach them that I am at the door for one reason only—to greet them and let them know I am glad they are there. After the first week of this, they eagerly look for me to be at the door to welcome them. My students know that if for some reason I am not at the door, they should seek me out to receive their morning greeting before heading to their seats.

I also train my students to speak to me both when they leave the room and when they return. It's amazing how many students go through each school day without getting the one-on-one recognition that is so vital to getting them to connect. This should never happen.

I find this simple technique very effective at getting my students excited about being at school. Former students who have moved on to higher grades often tell me how much they miss this personal touch.

2

Say Good-bye at the End of Each Day

Lessons in basic greetings are important in helping students develop social skills. The practice of saying good-bye at the end of each day goes right along with greeting students in the morning. I never let my students go home for the day without giving them that one-on-one moment where we say good-bye and wish one another a good afternoon.

During my third year in the classroom, one of my students died very unexpectedly in a tragic accident. Don Jones had brilliant red hair and freckles and was a little shy and timid when he entered my fifth-grade class. Our school was planning a talent show for the teachers and students that year, and after much effort, I convinced Don to try out for the show by performing an impression of the lead singer of Simply Red, a popular band in the late 1980s. Several students in the class were preparing talent show acts, and I wanted Don to take part in the excitement. The Friday before spring break, announcements about the talent show were made over the public address system, and we learned that every student in my class who had entered an act had been selected, including Don.

I will never forget the excitement that lit up Don's face when he heard his name called. What a way to begin spring break! I didn't know it at the time, but that Friday afternoon when I hugged Don and said good-bye, it was to be forever. Don lost his life in a drowning accident the Thursday of spring break. I still think of him often, and I will always remember our last moment together, one filled with joy and elation for the both of us.

3

The Power of Touch

Dr. Leo Buscaglia, a popular author and educator known best for his message of love, has greatly influenced my understanding of the power of human touch. Changes in our society have led many educators to discourage the practice of hugging students, but within the boundaries of professionalism and wisdom, I am very affectionate with my students. I've been hugging students my entire teaching career.

Each morning I greet my students with a hug, and each afternoon I say good-bye with a hug. There's a whole lot of hugging throughout the day as well. It's just my way of saying I love you no matter what you look like or dress like or whether you did your homework last night. Love is unconditional, and I have found no better way to express it than with a big hug. I am not advocating that everybody be a hugger, but I would suggest that you at least develop some sort of fancy handshake or hand jive that lets you get close to your students. I often do both.

Leo Buscaglia was sometimes called Dr. Hug because he had a tradition of hugging everyone who attended his speaking engagements. I had the pleasure of hearing him speak when he visited Atlanta in the late 1980s. I joined the multitude of audience members who waited in line for at least an hour to receive a hug from the "Doctor of Hug." The following Monday, I told my students about my experience, and they were quite impressed. Later that school year they threw a surprise birthday party for me, which culminated with all thirty-five of them forming a line to give me a big birthday hug. Leo Buscaglia would have been proud, and probably a little bit envious.

4

Eat Lunch with Your Students

Throughout my teaching career I have always enjoyed eating lunch with my students instead of at the teachers' table. Everyone has an opinion about this practice—some people argue that students need downtime away from their teachers—and I respect them all.

My students love it when I eat with them. We are able to talk about things not tied to academics. I find out about their hobbies, families, problems, and so forth. These times are precious, and vital to helping me bond with my students.

I usually move around at lunchtime so that I can hang out with different students during the week. My students are also able to receive academic help during lunch if they request it. We often eat in the classroom, which also helps us connect as a family. Sharing a meal as friends encourages a higher level of social intimacy and closeness.

Since I became coordinator of our school's chess club and started using chess in my daily math instruction, we have established the tradition of playing chess during our lunch period each day. Our lunch chess games allow my students to get to know each other better because the chess computer program we use chooses their opponents.

5

The Power of Play

I learned early on in life the power of play. As far back as I can remember, my father always participated in whatever activity my siblings and I were engaged in, instead of just being a spectator. Even today as he approaches the age of eighty, he would still rather play than watch. My brothers and I are often on the losing end in our family bowling outings.

Because of my background in sports and physical education, it is very natural for me during recess to find myself the quarterback for both teams in a pickup football game or the pitcher for both teams in softball or kickball. Lately I have been learning to play soccer, the current number one sport at our school. Whether it is jumping rope, playing dodge ball, swinging on the playground, or running laps, students really appreciate my involvement.

Whatever activity we are involved in, I require all my students to participate. I want every child to have the benefit of being part of the team and getting some exercise. Thanks to our focus on physical activity, we usually do well on field day.

So get off the fence and get involved. Your students are going to love it, and you'll love it too. Playing is not just for kids.

6

Laugh with Your Students

Don't be afraid to let your students see you laugh. I have always found it kind of funny when I encounter teachers who never laugh in the classroom. My classroom is always full of laughter.

Do be careful, however, that no one in your classroom ever laughs at someone else's expense. Students know the difference between someone laughing with them and someone laughing at them. My students and I do sometimes poke friendly fun at one another, but never until we have been together for a couple of months, and never with a mean spirit. The writer of Proverbs was correct when he said, "Laughter doeth good like a medicine."

7

Smile a Lot

Back in the early '80s when I started my teaching career, there was a very popular saying among educators that went something like, "Don't let them see you smile till Christmas."

This advice was primarily given to help teachers develop control and discipline—a stern face equals a disciplined class. I address control and discipline elsewhere in this book, but just so you know where I stand, I don't believe a stern face has anything to do with discipline.

I have won over many students and parents with a simple, warm smile. A smile means you're happy, and every student wants a happy teacher.

8

Become a Storyteller

Tell me a fact, and I will learn. Tell me a truth, and I will believe. But tell me a story, and it will live in my heart forever.

Most good teachers are also good storytellers. Everybody likes a good story, and even teachers who have been on the job for just a few years have stories to tell. Most of the stories I tell involve either things that have happened to me in my personal life or things I have experienced in the classroom.

My stories are sometimes planned and at other times completely spontaneous. They are designed to instruct, motivate, and, of course, create laughter. My students love to listen to my stories mainly because they are true. They also know that in the future they may become the main character in one of my stories.

9

Be Wild and Crazy

"Mr. A, you're so crazy!" If your students have never called you crazy (in a nice way), then I suggest you liven things up a bit. I have been called crazy for my raps, dances, practical jokes, drama, and other wacky techniques.

At the beginning of the year, my students are really not quite ready for my uniqueness, and they often don't know how to handle me. As the year moves on, however, they begin to adapt to my "craziness."

So get a little nutty every now and then. You will have more fun, and your students will too. Being a teacher is being part entertainer.

10

Make Friendly Challenges

I love to give my students friendly challenges. My most recent challenge involved reading. We have a great reading incentive program at Norcross called Accelerated Reader. In this program, students read a variety of books and can then collect points by taking computer-based comprehension tests. Each year we set a goal for how many points we can earn as a class.

Friendly challenges can be as creative as you let them. After I initiated the concept of book clubs with my students this year, they began to read like crazy. Since everybody was becoming wild about reading, I decided to add some fuel to the fire. I challenged them to double, in one week, the amount of points they had acquired over the past two weeks. If they reached this goal, I would dye my beard blond and keep it that way for a week. That blond beard aged me almost twenty years, and that week was the longest seven days I have ever experienced. I had to send an e-mail to my colleagues to let them know that I had not completely lost my mind. We won't get into how often I had to explain my new look to people I ran into in the Norcross community.

Friendly challenges can create unity among your students as they work toward a common goal. If you lose your challenge, in the spirit of fair play you have to accept your consequence; likewise, so do your students.

11

Talk with Your Students

I have always enjoyed just relaxing and talking with my students. I am typically much taller than my students, so to avoid intimidating them, I make it a practice to get down on their level when speaking with them.

Talking with students helps them feel important and interesting. My students feel comfortable having conversations with me about almost anything. I love it when I am able to get a normally shy and timid student to open up and talk to me.

In addition to talking with my own students, I love to speak to students I see walking down the hall or passing my classroom. A simple "Good morning," "Hello," or "How are you?" can make a student's day. Everybody has a need to be recognized. I gain a lot of favor with students who are not in my classroom simply because I take the time to speak to them.

At a local soccer game recently, a young man in his twenties approached me to ask if I was Mr. A, a teacher at Norcross. He told me that he was a former Norcross student who had started at the school in the middle of the year. He could not remember who his fifth-grade teacher was, but he remembered me, he said, because I had spoken to him as he walked down the hall. I had complimented him on the shirt he was wearing, which read "Mexicans are Cool."

Our students remember our words forever, which means we have to govern and control our tongue. Just as the writer of Proverbs advises us in the area of laughter, he also reminds us that *life and death are in the power of the tongue* (Proverbs 18:21). When we communicate with our students, our words need to produce life, not death.

12

Listen to Your Students

We have two ears and one mouth; therefore, we should listen twice as much as we talk. This little saying is true not only when it comes to gaining favor from our students, but in life as well.

Being a good listener takes practice and a lot of work. It means I have to stop what I am doing, face my students, and give them my attention. I constantly have to remind myself that people are more important than things. When I show my students this through my actions, I gain a tremendous amount of favor with them.

There are moments when I tell my students that I need a little downtime and will not be available for a while. I do this in a variety of ways. Sometimes I wear my ball cap to signal to my students that I need some uninterrupted time to myself.

13

Incorporate Letter Writing

Letter writing is a great way to encourage students, especially those who are shy, to express themselves a little more. Two or three times a year I assign students the task of writing a letter to me. They are allowed to tell me anything in these letters. They are also permitted to ask me questions.

I write back to each student with a thoughtful response to his or her letter, which is the most important part of this activity. Yes, it takes some time and effort, but it is definitely worth the investment. My students become so elated when they get their letter back from me.

Remember to always use discretion when writing to your students. There should be no problem with students sharing their letters with their parents or other family members.

Kyrie Lantz, a former student of mine, moved to Arkansas after her fifth-grade year. Even though I have not seen Kyrie in seven years, she continues to write to me two or three times a year, and her mom sends Christmas pictures along with the letters. Through these letters and pictures, I have been able to watch Kyrie grow up to become a wonderful young lady.

14

Write Personal Notes to Parents and Students

Send positive notes home to your students' parents. You can write these in agenda books or in the "notes to parents" booklets that most school-related stores carry. Parents love to receive positive information about their children.

I also write notes to my students encouraging them to work harder or praising them for something positive they accomplished. My students always smile and feel good about themselves when I send them notes, even if they're of a corrective nature. It is widely believed that written notes of encouragement are more genuine and powerful than spoken words.

Give note-writing a try, and watch the positive results it will yield.

15

Learn as Much about Each Student as You Can

Make an effort to get to know your students. Each student is special, and it is up to you to know your students' likes, dislikes, hobbies, dreams, family situation, and so forth. I have found that the more I know about my students, the more I am able to help them achieve in the classroom. The more I know, the more avenues I have to motivate them to do their best.

The more you know about your students, the more you will find out how different they really are. They cannot all be treated the same. You have to treat them differently because they are different.

I recall a former student who was taking a timed standardized writing test. He was not working fast enough, and I needed him to pick up the pace. After trying several times to urge him on, I decided to use a basketball phrase—he was a basketball player—I knew he would be familiar with. I whispered in his ear, "Take the ball to the hole, son! Take the ball to the hole!" He peered up at me and smiled, then immediately picked up the pace and completed the test in the allotted time. Know your students!

16

Visit Your Students' Homes

I make it a point to know where each of my students lives. Home visiting is a strategy I have used my entire teaching career. My home visits have a variety of purposes. These include, among other things, visiting students who are ill, checking on students who are absent, holding parent conferences, and attending birthday parties and festivals.

My students always get excited when I visit them at home. One home visit I made a few years back was academics related—the student was not working as hard as I knew he could. This student was so excited I had stopped by his house that he could not stop smiling, even while I was telling his dad how he wasn't completing all his homework and schoolwork or performing up to his ability level. He thought my visit was the coolest thing, even though it was of a corrective nature.

17

Live Where You Teach

Several of my colleagues would advise you not to live in the community you teach in, and I respect their opinion. But I was raised in a small town where everyone knew everyone else. Both of my parents were schoolteachers in the community I grew up in, and I saw firsthand how effective and respected they were as teachers and involved citizens in the community.

Being part of the community allows me to connect better with the students and families who are part of my daily life. I have lived in the community I teach in for my entire career, and I have no regrets. I can be seen all over town—at the post office, grocery store, and especially along my favorite jogging route.

18

Attend Extracurricular Activities

Living in the community I teach in makes it easier to support my students in their nonacademic endeavors. I try to attend sporting events, recitals, and other extracurricular performances as much as I can.

I find it particularly exciting to see former students progress and mature in their academic and nonacademic activities. Students and parents really appreciate the extra interest I take in their lives.

19

Attend Graduations and Special Occasions

Even after your students move on to other schools, try to attend their graduation ceremonies. I have had the pleasure of attending several high school and college graduation ceremonies during my career. Graduations are particularly special for me because of the many years that pass between fifth grade and the end of high school.

I had the wonderful experience, a few years ago, of being invited to the high school graduation of a favorite student of mine, Amit Momaya. Listening to Amit give the salutatorian's address was an incredible experience!

Another graduation invitation I will always remember came from another favorite student of mine, Alan Michaels. Alan had only a limited number of tickets to his graduation ceremony, but he made a special visit to Norcross Elementary just to give me one. His words move me even today. "I told my mom that you were getting a ticket to my graduation," he said, "even if it means that my grandparents won't." I was completely overwhelmed. What an honor and tribute!

I also attended Alan's graduation from Georgia Tech and spent the day with his family celebrating his achievements. I always make it a point to respond to the graduation announcements I receive from former students who no longer live in the area. It feels great to be remembered.

20

Give Students Your Phone Number

Giving students my phone number is a great way to help them communicate with me, especially former students who have moved away. It's always a special moment when I get a phone call from a former student who wants to see how I'm doing and share what is happening in his or her life.

Use your own wisdom with this tip. I allow current students to call for assistance with school-related activities or just to say hello. If I happen to be busy, I simply ask them to call back later.

Jermaine Holloway, a former student of mine who is currently serving in Iraq with the marines, frequently calls me on Father's Day. Two years ago I received a very special phone call from Paula Delgado, a student who had emigrated from Mexico at the age of six. The summer after her fifth-grade year, she had the opportunity to return to her country of birth and get in touch with her roots. I will never forget the excitement and joy I heard in her voice when she phoned me from Mexico to tell me about her trip.

A few years back I received a phone call around 11:30 PM from Janet Rodriguez, one of the students in my class at that time. Janet was crying hysterically because she had just learned that her entire family had been involved in an automobile accident. Fortunately no one was seriously injured. Janet simply needed someone to comfort her. She would never have been able to reach me if she had not known my phone number.

21

Be Transparent

Most students can spot a fake a mile away. I have always tried to be transparent and real with my students. They can count on me to be the same person whether they see me in the classroom, out in the community, or in their neighborhood.

I make sure my students know that I am not perfect. I tell them I am really just like their parents but that I happen to teach for a living. People are usually a little surprised to find out that I'm a teacher—I'm not anything like the teachers they had when they were in school. I love this response and always take it as a compliment.

With me, what you see is what you get. I don't want to confuse my students, so I don't give off mixed signals.

22

Keep Your Word

I make it a practice to keep my word to my students, but I am always careful when I promise them we are going to do something. I know they will lose confidence in me and in what I say if I repeatedly fail to fulfill my word to them.

Several times I have had to rearrange my schedule to fit in a special project or play that I had promised my students we were going to do. Keeping my word is also important when I accept invitations to attend extracurricular activities. My students would be very disappointed if I failed to show up for functions I promised to attend. I have often overheard my students commenting on the fact that I always keep my word, and that if I said we were going to do something, then we would do it. This really makes me feel good inside. A person is only as good as his or her word.

23

Invite Students to Your Home

At the end of each school year, I invite several students to my house for a cook-out. I started these yearly cookouts early in my teaching career and continue them today. Their basic purpose is to show my students where I live and make them aware that I am just a regular person.

The cookout is usually small and involves year-long honor students and chess team members. After I won the Milken Family Foundation National Educator Award in 1998, I invited my whole class to celebrate the special year we had.

These cookouts give me a great chance to show my transparency. My students are always excited to see where I live and what my house looks like on the inside. We spend the majority of the time out back in the hot tub and sliding on a water slide. Parents are welcome to attend, but they don't have to stay unless they want to.

I also occasionally have students over to do yard work or gardening projects, and we sometimes hold special chess team practice sessions at my house as well.

24

Share Your Goals with Your Students

I love to talk to my students about what's going on in my life. I don't share everything, of course, but I do share quite a bit. I always involve my students in my goals and dreams, and they often ask about my progress on a particular goal.

For my first marathon, a distance of 26.2 miles, my students all signed the sweat towel I carried with me during the race. Without that towel and the promise I made to those kids to finish that race, I never would have made it. My first marathon was brutal. I have since run three more, finally attaining my goal of completing the course in less than four hours.

My students also checked on my progress from time to time and held me accountable while I was writing this book.

25

Post Your Diplomas and Awards

Post your diplomas and awards in your room so that students and parents can see them. This is not to show how great you are, but rather to show students and parents that you are a competent teacher. This will give them confidence in your ability to educate. Doctors and other professionals do it, so why not teachers? When I look at my wall of awards, I am motivated to continue to work to the level I received recognition for in the first place.

I don't teach for awards, and I don't need them to feel validated. Truthfully, I was a little embarrassed by all the attention that came with receiving the Milken National Educator Award.

26

The Only Reason Is You

Your students must know that they are the sole reason you come to school each day. I frequently let my students know that "the only reason is you." I tell them over and over that without them I would have no job. I encourage my students to ask me lots of questions, raise their hands for assistance often, and make me work hard to earn my pay.

With the many non-teaching-related tasks I have to do each day, I could easily lose sight of my primary purpose. I have to remind myself from time to time that the schools were built for the students, not the teachers. My children must come first. They are the only reason I entered the teaching profession.

27

Physically Demonstrate the Concept of Team/Coach

Most students see the student-teacher relationship as students against teacher. I make sure my students know that's not really the case, and that we are actually on the same team. I am the coach, and every coach wants his or her team to win and achieve success.

At the beginning of each year, usually on the first day of school, I give my students a simple illustration of what my role as teacher will be for the year. I physically move from the front of the room to where they are seated and tell them, "It's us against whatever gets in our way this year. We are a team. I am the coach. I am going to help you because I am on your side. I am going to support you and help you achieve your dreams and goals." Once my students understand that we are heading in the same direction, they can make real progress.

28

Do Things Outside the School Setting

From time to time I like to get away from the school to interact with my students in a new setting. Going fishing, visiting theme parks, playing soccer, going out for pizza, visiting a bookstore, and attending sporting events are some of the things I do outside of the school setting with my students.

I have seen my students' eyes light up on their first trip to Six Flags to ride a roller coaster. I saw the excitement on the face of D. J. Stowe, a former student, after he bowled a score of more than 200 in a bowling league. I saw the sparkle in Paula Delgado's eyes when she had her picture taken with a famous Mexican national soccer player, and also while she led her soccer team in goals scored. I never would have had the opportunity to witness these and numerous other events if my relationship with my students had been kept inside the four walls of our classroom.

29

Encourage Your Students to Join Clubs

Norcross Elementary offers a variety of clubs. I feel it is vitally important that my students be involved in some sort of club or group activity. Students need to take part in some extracurricular activity that keeps them connected to a group. I honestly believe that is why we are losing so many good kids to gangs. It has been shown that most kids who join gangs don't already belong to a group that makes them feel accepted and affirmed. Every student wants to be a part of something, and if we don't provide reasonable alternatives, they will seek acceptance elsewhere. At Norcross students can participate in a range of organized clubs, including chess, math, chorus, art, drama, step team, dance team, soccer, and Spanish. Encourage your students to get involved in clubs or team sports.

30

Always Celebrate Birthdays

Few days are more special to a kid than his or her birthday. Fortunately, school birthday celebrations don't require a lot of effort. You don't need much more than a cupcake (with a candle, of course), a cool pencil, an ice cream, and a card signed by everyone in the class. A colleague of mine shared with me the idea of tying helium-inflated birthday balloons to the students' desks on their special day, and this has gone over very well. It's always neat to watch a birthday student peer into the classroom in search of balloons. With all the dollar stores around these days, birthday balloons have become very affordable. In my class we also celebrate summer birthdays, so that no student gets left out. Some students with summer birthdays reach fifth grade never having celebrated their birthday with their classmates.

We normally sing "Happy Birthday" in English and Spanish since the largest ethnicity-based population in our school is Hispanic. I do allow parents to bring in cupcakes or other treats if they would like to do something special for their child.

About eight years ago my students and I started a great tradition for celebrating my birthday. During my career I have had my share of (supposedly) surprise birthday parties, but the new tradition involves me throwing my own party.

About a week before my birthday eight years back, I was at the board teaching, watching the clock because as usual I was running out of time. There are just not enough hours in each day to teach. This particular day, I turned to my students and told them that what I really wanted on my birthday was to just disregard the dismissal bell and teach two extra hours, and afterward head for Lupita's, a local Mexican restaurant, to eat a few tacos. I said this as a joke of course, but my students said, "Yes, we'll do it." So a tradition was born.

Each year to celebrate my birthday, my students remain after school and allow me to teach whatever I desire. Several of my former students meet us at the restaurant later. I can think of no better way to celebrate my birthday than by having my students around me. It is always nice to see the different grade levels interact with one another. One student, Melissa Johnson, who is now a senior in high school, has attended every celebration since she was in my class. Her loyalty is amazing. My students and I always look forward to my annual birthday bash.

31

Find Ways to Brag about Your Students

We all like to hear good things about ourselves. Students are no different. I love to brag about my students in front of other teachers and in front of their classmates. I might brag about the whole class or one student, and my compliments can focus on academics, behavior, or people skills. Bragging is a great way to let students know how pleased you are with them.

It is always wonderful to see the shining faces of students who've heard me compliment them. I teach my students not to brag about themselves, but to let others take care of that. If they are good at something, they won't have to tell anyone, because people will tell them.

32

Be a Student Advocate

My students are the only reason I teach—it's important that I be an advocate for them. I support them in any way I can and always try to see things from their point of view. I listen when they suggest ways that things can be done better, and I back them in trying to get things changed.

I also follow the progress of my former students, and I am always ready to speak on their behalf if needed. I want my students to know they can depend on me. I have written reference letters, sent e-mails, made phone calls, received calls from jail, attended court hearings for students who have gotten off track, and provided transportation for families. Life can be tough, and it's important that students have someone to count on.

33

Teach Your Students How to Gain Favor

This book describes techniques you can use to gain favor with your students. It's also important to teach students how to gain favor with others. In my opinion, the number one way I can help students gain favor with adults is to teach them people skills. Respectful and polite kids impress most adults because what was considered commonplace years ago in the area of manners is so rare with today's students.

To help them adapt to me, I let my students know what pleases me and what my pet peeves are. Gaining favor with me is pretty easy. Once my students understand my expectations, they can choose either to gain my favor or lose it. Please understand that favor has nothing to do with the quality of education my students receive. I educate them regardless of how they behave.

I also teach my students how to gain favor with future teachers and other people they will meet throughout their lives.

34

Teach People Skills

People skills are the most important skills I teach my students. We begin working on people skills during our first encounter, which is usually on registration day, the Thursday before the first day of school. The first thing I teach my students is to use the words *Sir* and *Ma'am* and *Yes* and *No* when addressing me or any other adult. It takes some time and gentle guidance, but the students catch on.

I am a big believer in teaching students to respect one another. I expect them to use words and phrases such as "Please," "Thank you," "Excuse me," and "I am sorry. Please forgive me." I love to hear my students say thank you to one another when distributing or passing out materials.

Bus drivers on field trips always get a kick out of my students' good manners. After a hayride at Burt's Pumpkin Farm a few years back, the driver of the tractor told me that my class was the best group he'd ever taken on a hayride in all his years working for Burt's. My students had acted no differently during the ride than any other students would. What impressed the driver was the "Thank you" each student gave when the ride was over. The driver was not used to that kind of treatment. Courtesy like this is not as commonplace as I feel it should be, and students have to be taught that it's important.

One of my classroom rules is that boys must always allow girls to enter the room first. I teach my boys how to conduct themselves as gentlemen and my girls to conduct themselves as ladies.

I assign one member of my class to act as door holder each week, and my students are trained to say "Thank you" to him or her. I often remind them that the door is not holding itself, that there's a person connected to it.

Throughout the year my students really catch on and make great improvement in relating to one another. It really makes me feel good when another teacher notices my students respecting one another and the other adults in our school. It also gives me great pleasure when my students take ownership and begin to remind one another to use appropriate people skills.

These people skills are meant to last a lifetime, not just one school year. Having all the academic skills in the world means nothing if you can't relate to those around you. It's been said that the number one reason people lose their jobs or fail to be promoted is their lack of people skills.

A mother once asked Gandhi to get her son to stop eating sugar. Gandhi told the child, "Come back in two weeks." Two weeks later the mother brought the child before Gandhi. Gandhi said to the boy, "Stop eating sugar." Puzzled, the woman replied, "Thank you, but I must ask you, why didn't you tell him that two weeks ago?" Gandhi replied, "Two weeks ago I was eating sugar."

I know I can't expect my students to use people skills if I don't model these skills in front of them every day. I always ask permission before borrowing something from a student, and before sharing students' writing or ideas with the class. I never ask something of my students that I don't practice myself.

35

Trick and Treat Your Kids

I mentioned earlier how important humor and laughter are in the classroom. I also believe in the power of a treat. I remember my mother buying treats for her second-grade students. I always thought the treats were just for my sister and me. It wasn't until I became a teacher myself that I discovered my mom had been practicing the technique of treating students.

I don't use treats for behavior modification. My treats are just another way of saying, "I love you, and I want to do something nice for you." I don't have an organized plan for treating students; I just know by experience when it's needed. I have used food, extra recess time, no homework, and extra silent reading time as treats. I also traditionally treat my students to ice cream the Friday of the first week of school to wrap up our first days together. There's really nothing so sweet as a treat.

36

Have Former Students Give Testimonials

Throughout my career I have been blessed to have former students return to see me. I always use these visits to have the older students speak to my current students. These testimonials are incredibly powerful.

What a thrill for me to hear my former students encourage my current students with the same words and messages I used to encourage them when they were in my class! Words carry so much power. I am careful with what I say and how I say it because I know my students will remember my words, positive or negative.

I always let my current students know that the student standing before them was once a fifth grader just like they are now. My older students serve as great mentors for my current students.

The best thing students can say about you is that something you said or did had a positive influence on them. Hearing from former students always brings me joy.

Toward the end of this book, I share some messages from my students in a special section called "In Their Own Words."

37

Treat Your Students with Respect

I know that if I don't respect my students, they will have no respect for me. Respect has nothing to do with age. Everybody, whether young or old, needs to be treated with respect. Students need to be affirmed and lifted up.

I use the same people skills with my students that I ask them to use with me. I say "Thank you." I ask them if it's OK to borrow their pencil or book or share their work or idea with the class.

The most important part of gaining respect from my students is admitting when I am wrong. Whenever I mishandle a discipline situation or make a mistake, I apologize in front of the class to the students involved and ask their forgiveness. This sets an example for my students and helps the class to feel closer.

38

Be Loyal

I strive each year to be loyal to my students. I let them know they can count on me to be there for them. Through the years I have discovered that if I am fiercely loyal to my students, they will be fiercely loyal to me.

I can count on my students for anything I need, and they are always ready to help when I ask something of them. This loyalty continues after our year together in the classroom ends. I saw this two years ago while helping students prepare for the Georgia State Scholastic Chess Tournament. I am involved with both the elementary and middle school chess teams. Unfortunately some of my best players give up chess after leaving my class. The state tournament is very competitive, and I knew we would need the assistance of some of these former players. One simple phone call to Janet Rodriguez and Anna Medrano, two of my former top players, was all it took. I mentioned to Janet and Anna that I needed them to start playing again to strengthen the Summerour Middle School team. They both showed up for the next practice session, no questions asked, and were a vital part of our success. The relationship between us left little doubt on my part that the girls would join the team. That's loyalty!

39

Be Accessible and Approachable

I want my students to know that I am approachable and accessible. Once they respect me as a listener, they will begin to share more of themselves. I don't want my students to be afraid to approach me with their problems. If I am not accessible or they sense that I am not interested, they will seek others who are, mainly their peers, who are often clueless when it comes to offering advice and finding solutions to problems.

It is extremely tough being a kid these days. My students struggle with a variety of issues. They need to know I care about them and that they have worth. Once they see me as approachable, they seek me out and allow me to speak words of encouragement and truth into their lives to help them make sense of the world.

40

Love and Accept All Your Students

I may not like everything my students do and say, but I still love them as people. I let them see that I love *all* of them, not just the ones who are the most physically attractive or have the best clothes. Our students will accept the students we accept and reject the ones we reject.

Love is unconditional. It has nothing to do with performance and behavior, but everything to do with being a person. I strive to make sure that all my students know, without a doubt, that I love them for who they are. I teach them that they have something to offer to our class and the world.

This concept is easier said than done, but students who don't feel loved and cared for will never give all they have. On the other hand, students who feel loved will return the favor by trying to move mountains to please you.

41

The Strength of the Pack

Rudyard Kipling wrote in *The Jungle Book*, "For the strength of the pack is the wolf, and the strength of the wolf is the pack." This is one of my favorite quotations. I use it quite frequently during the year to emphasize to my students that if we as a team are to be successful, we must treat every member of the class as important. Each student has to know that he or she is a vital part of the team.

I accomplish this in part by assigning class jobs. My students take turns serving as paper distributors, door holders, and table washers, to name a few. Don't let the smart and physically attractive students do everything. As I said, every student needs to be a part of the team. The stronger the individual members are, the stronger the class will be. The strength of the class is the student, and the strength of the student is the class.

42

Communicate with Parents on a Regular Basis

This tip deals more with gaining favor from parents, which is vital to students' success. I try to communicate with my students' parents by phone as well as through regular progress checks.

Parents really want answers to three questions:

1. How is my child progressing academically in comparison with the other students?

2. How is my child behaving?

3. How is my child progressing socially?

I have found regular phone calls to be quite effective. The calls I make to brag about a student are the most powerful. All parents love hearing something good about their child. I suggest the very first phone call you make for each student, when possible, should be about something the student has done well rather than vice versa.

43

Celebrate Academic Achievement and Perfect Attendance

Ask any of my students, and they will tell you that I love to celebrate! After each grading period we always have a celebration for students who make the honor roll or have perfect attendance. This is in addition to what we do as a grade level. Honor students usually remain after school for a pizza or hotdog party and playtime. We also have a special candlelight lunch in the classroom. The candlelight lunches require very little preparation, and the students love them. Students with perfect attendance also have a lunchtime celebration. We always look forward to our special time together.

Occasionally I will invite to lunch a student who might not have made the honor roll, but who improved dramatically during the grading period. I feel strongly about recognizing improvement.

44

Get Your Class Recognized

At some point during the year I try to have my students recognized in the local newspaper. When students read an article about themselves or see their own faces in the paper, they really feel good about themselves.

If we are doing an interesting project, I simply call the newspaper to see if they could send someone out to publicize it. It's a good idea to develop a relationship with the local education reporter. I also write my own news stories and send them into the paper. We have had reading and community service projects, creative dance programs, chess club results, and other successes and activities recognized in the newspaper.

45

Purchase Class T-shirts

To promote unity and team spirit among my students, I order class T-shirts each year. Our class shirts not only help us to look like a team, they are designed to spread the word about reading for pleasure. On the front of the shirts is a reading slogan I created, "W.ild A.bout R.eading," and on the back there's a statement that reads, "Activate Your Mind—Read!" A former student, Lera Buettner, designed our shirt in 1995 while a member of my class, and we still use her design today.

On specially chosen days throughout the year, everyone in my class wears their class reading shirt. We always wear them on field day. They also come in handy on field trips and activities away from the school—even in a crowd I can identify my students. We draw a lot of attention because of how good we look!

46

Be a Positive Role Model

When I was a boy growing up in the small town of Tallapoosa, Georgia, I had a Sunday schoolteacher by the name of Mrs. Matty L. McCauley, who always encouraged us to be good role models. She often said that no matter how well or badly we conducted ourselves, there was always someone looking at us wishing to be just like us. I carried this piece of advice into adulthood, and I continue to live by it today.

My students like to imitate me in big and little things. If I roll my sleeve in a certain way, it won't be long until the boys in my class start to roll their sleeves the same way. If I treat a student as unimportant, it won't be long until the other students begin to do the same. If I ridicule a student's response, so will my students.

Living in the same community as my students also means I have to be prudent in my personal life. I don't ever want to lead a student, past or former, astray through my actions. As a teacher, I try to conduct myself in a manner that will give those students who want to be just like me something positive to look at. Educators are in a position of influence. We are role models whether we want to be or not.

47

Learn Another Language

My school has a large population of ESOL students, many of whom are Hispanic. I began to learn Spanish several years ago, so I could speak to the few Hispanic students we had at the time. Little did I know that our school demographics would undergo such drastic change, and become the way they are today.

What started out as a simple hobby has turned into one of my greatest teaching tools. Being able to speak Spanish helps me relate to my Hispanic students. More importantly, it lets me communicate more effectively with their parents, who are sometimes reluctant to get involved in the school community because of the language barrier.

I love to see the surprised smiles emerge on the faces of students and parents when I speak to them in their native language. They are so appreciative of having a teacher they can communicate with, but are even more thankful for my efforts to learn their language.

48

Take and Post Lots of Pictures

I suggest you invest in the purchase of a digital camera and take lots of pictures of your students throughout the year. I create PowerPoint presentations of all our major projects and field trips. During parent conferences I run the presentations continuously so that parents can see the types of learning activities students are involved in. These PowerPoint presentations are always fun to view on the last day of school because fifth-grade students change so much during the year.

I post pictures in the classroom and on a bulletin board in the hallway. A colleague gave me the wonderful idea of creating a month-by-month picture timeline of classroom events. This is a neat and aesthetically pleasing way to showcase what we do in our class.

I also post class pictures in the room so that my students can see my former classes. Above the pictures are the words "All My Children." Former students always head to that section of the room whenever they drop by for a visit. My current students have fun trying to pick out the older students as they were in fifth grade.

49

Send Pictures Home

As I mentioned earlier, I take pictures throughout the year. Lately I have begun to send home pictures of my students involved in a variety of learning activities. I attach a short note to the pictures I send. The reaction from parents has been very positive. For really special occasions (when students receive awards, for example), I send the pictures enclosed in small frames I buy at the dollar store.

50

Display Quotations throughout the Room

I have always been fond of words and quotations, and it is quite natural for me to share this love with my students. I have found it quite helpful to create small posters to display motivating quotations throughout the classroom for students to read. Some of my favorites are listed below:

1. Somewhere, something incredible is waiting to happen.
2. For the strength of the pack is the wolf, and the strength of the wolf is the pack.
3. Who will dare to be great?
4. You will always repeat what you remember.
5. The desire to succeed means nothing without the desire to practice.
6. Excellence is never an accident.
7. Success takes *we'll* power.
8. We are what we repeatedly do. Excellence, then, is not an act but a habit.
9. A person who does not read has no real advantage over a person who cannot read.
10. Sometimes focus and effort are greater than talent.
11. Someone is practicing when you are not. When you play them, they will beat you.
12. The deep calls the deep.
13. Launch out into the deep.
14. Don't spectate. Participate.
15. You were born to win.
16. What you do today determines your tomorrow.
17. Attitude is everything.
18. Hard work beats talent when talent does not work hard.
19. Practice makes permanent! Perfect practice makes perfect!
20. It is not about being tired, it's about performance.
21. Preparation prevents poor performance.
22. Aguántate tantito y la fruta caerá en tu mano.

23. Echale pa' alante.

24. Si se puede.

25. Aquel que hoy se cae, se levantará mañana.

Quotations are a great way to send positive messages to students. My students see them day after day. I know they are effective when I hear my students use them on a regular basis.

51

Have Pets in the Room

I frequently have students at my school come up and ask me if I really have a snake in my classroom. I have loved animals since I was a young child and had a variety of pets when I was growing up. During my career I have tried several pets in the classroom. Some of them, such as hamsters and rabbits, required a level of care that created quite a lot of work for the students and me.

For the last six to seven years I have chosen low-maintenance pets, including a garter snake by the name of Jake the Snake and a salamander called Sally. My students—girls and boys—love to hold Jake. They find him quite interesting, especially when he eats and sheds. Jake eats live feeder fish, and he is a superb entertainer when it's feeding time. I also keep a bucket of mealworms that I have maintained for ten years or more.

I teach my students how to feed the pets, clean their cages, and perform other animal-related duties. I also use pets during science instruction when we study life science.

Needless to say, thanks to my snake and bucket of worms, the custodians are not very enthusiastic about cleaning my room. If you ever hear screams coming from my room, it's not me doing the screaming!

52

Create a Warm Atmosphere

I strive to create a warm, friendly class environment. I want my students to feel comfortable expressing themselves and asking questions. I have a huge sign in my room that reads, "It's intelligent to ask questions."

I often have visitors comment on the warm, friendly atmosphere in my room. It's not always neat and tidy (I can hear the custodians saying amen to that), but it is student friendly. We have several comfortable reading chairs, and I use plug-in air fresheners—vanilla is my favorite—to give the room an inviting smell. If you have pets in the room, air freshener is a must.

I love it when my students say they wish the school day would never end. When I hear this, I know I am doing a good job of creating the right atmosphere.

A warm atmosphere is also important because for some of my students, the classroom is the only place they can find refuge from the many issues that surround their lives.

53

Lights! Camera! Action!

Drama is not just for the drama club. I do several plays and performance activities with my students each year. Plays allow us to practice reading in a fun and exciting way. They promote reading fluency because students have to read through their lines several times to memorize them. They also expose students to a plethora of new vocabulary words. I use plays that involve all the students and have enough roles for everyone. This allows us to work together as a team toward a common goal.

Since we don't have an auditorium, we hang curtains in our room and transform it into a theater. We invite other classes to watch us perform.

I also use creative dance in our annual Grammar and Punctuation Raps. I try to incorporate the physical with the mental. Our yearly Black History Potpourri involves poetry, game songs, drama, and a tribute to Motown that gets my students singing and dancing and imitating the great Motown entertainers.

Students should not sit at their desks day after day doing paper work. Students have different ways of learning, so I adapt my style of teaching to fit their individual needs. Students who are gifted physically shine when they get to express themselves in a nonsedentary manner. I feel it is vitally important to let my students express themselves through creative dance and other nontraditional means.

54

Teach Poetry and Affirmations

I am a firm believer in teaching poetry and affirmations. I usually start the year with Langston Hughes's "Dreams" or Robert Frost's "The Road Not Taken." We tackle several other poems and poets as the year progresses. We closely study the poems we read and memorize to try to find out what message the author is trying to convey. Poems don't have to be of great length to carry a powerful message.

Of course, throughout the year we also write our own poems. I normally use the book *Poetry From Scratch*, by Michael Carey, as an introduction to writing poetry. I do allow my students to create rhyming poetry, but the bulk of my instruction is in free style, where the students get to make the decisions about rhythm and line breaks. We focus on showing rather than telling, and use lots of sense words. A great deal of our poems deal with the subject matter we are studying at the time. In the poem below, one of my students, Brittany Timpson, expresses her thoughts on the Roaring Twenties, a topic we cover in social studies.

Roaring '20s, Razz and Tazz

Can you hear it?
The slow jazz
Or all the razz and tazz
Slow, fast, slow, fast.
Music is running up
And down the street,
Screaming and hollering.
I feel like tapping my heels!
I feel like slipping and sliding!
I feel like jumping in the air!
I feel like gliding through the air
And
Coming back down to strong arms.
Can you hear the drums go
Boom! Boom! Boom!

It's ringing in my ear.

It'll never stop.

Several of my former students have mentioned to me that our fifth-grade poetry unit inspired them to get in touch with their poetic voice. Erika Harris, Michael Btembke, Lindsey Sumner, Anquenetta Kenon, Paula Delgado, and Brittany Timpson are examples of students who were able to get in touch with their poetic voice during our fifth-grade poetry unit. You can find poems by Michael and Paula in the "In Their Own Words" section of this book.

We have also initiated a poetry café, which we call our "Poetry Slam," where our classroom is transformed into a French café. We serve donuts and coffee, and my students showcase their poetry in a fun and exciting way.

Affirmations are another way to motivate and encourage our students with positive messages. I usually have my students echo me as I lead them in a particular affirmation. There are several resources with great affirmations, or you can simply create your own. An example of something I might use would be the following: "I am somebody. I am a thinker. I am a problem solver. The mind is my primary business. I know it does not matter where I come from, but what I come with. There is no obstacle that can hold me back or stand in my way. I will go around it, over it, under it, or through it to reach my destination."

55

Teach Goal Setting

It is crucial that we teach students how to set and attain goals. I feel that in many classrooms this is overlooked. Goal setting is a skill that students can carry with them throughout their lifetime.

I usually begin with academic goal setting and then branch off into other areas of student interest. The most important part of teaching goal setting is breaking the overall goal into daily workable parts. Success in goal setting usually comes by doing the little things over and over correctly.

Most students shy away from trying to read longer books. Once I show the students how to break books down into smaller chunks, they see that large books are no different than smaller books. They learn how setting and meeting short-range goals help them accomplish the long-range goal.

I model goal setting by showing my students how I set and reach my goals. I kept them up-to-date on my progress when I was training to run my first marathon, and showed them how with proper planning and discipline, great things can be accomplished.

56

Teach Your Students Chess

In Gwinnett County Public Schools, scholastic chess programs are growing more and more each year, with more students playing than ever before. If your school does not have a chess program, speak to your administrators about starting one.

About four years ago I was forced to learn this remarkable game when the chess coordinator at our school, Ben Pennington, transferred to another county and left the chess club in my hands. Since then I have fallen in love with the game, and I use it as a teaching tool almost daily.

Since I have incorporated chess into my math program, I have seen firsthand how it directly affects my students' abilities in problem solving, math, and other academic areas. As a direct result of playing chess, my students' analytical and logical reasoning skills have improved drastically. At our school students are very interested in learning the game. My students love it and would play all day if I let them.

True, chess does "make kids smarter." In addition it has also been shown to improve school attendance and behavior.

The Norcross Elementary competitive chess team competes in several tournaments every year and qualified for the Georgia Scholastic State Team Chess Tournament in 2003, 2004, and 2005. They scored their first positive score at the state tournament in 2004.

57

Do Not Teach behind a Desk

If you are a desk teacher, get yourself up, and get out among your students. Students are more likely to ask for assistance if you are moving among them rather than stuck in the front or back of the room. As you circulate, you should be constantly asking your students what you can do to help them.

I make sure that while my students are practicing a particular skill I am not grading papers or checking my e-mail. I am better able to give my students immediate feedback if I'm circulating throughout the room as they work.

It has been said one of the greatest motivators for students is feedback on performance. The sooner or more immediate the feedback, the greater influence it will have. You can't very well give prompt feedback if you're sitting at your desk.

58

Read to Your Students Each Day

My favorite part of the school day is the time I spend reading to my students. I love it! I owe my love of reading to my mom, and my love of reading aloud to Dr. Tom Davidson, one of my college professors.

On my very first night in Dr. D's reading class I listened to him read a book titled *Alexander and the Terrible, Horrible, No Good, Very Bad Day*. I had never in all my years had a book read to me the way Dr. D read *Alexander*. He made that book come alive, and I was immediately hooked.

My students always get excited when it is time for me to read aloud because I deliver each book like Dr. D delivered *Alexander*. Reading aloud is an art form that, with practice, anybody can learn. Make the book come alive. Give the characters different voices. Change your tone and volume. Mix up the tempo.

If you really want to try something fun, darken your classroom during the month of October and read to your students using a flashlight and microphone. Be sure to choose a scary book such as *The Dollhouse Murders* or *Wait Till Helen Comes*. I love to scare my fifth graders.

My former students often tell me that one of the things they miss most in language arts is the way I read to them aloud. You can find a list of some of my favorite read-aloud stories at the back of this book.

59

Be Enthusiastic

When I was nearing the end of my college studies, I learned one of the most valuable lessons I've ever had about teaching. I was a student teacher, and had just finished teaching a science lesson to a class of eighth graders, which was observed by my professor, Dr. Klee. As usual, Dr. Klee wanted to discuss the positive and negative points of my lesson. While sitting on the steps outside the school, we were interrupted by a teacher ranting and raving at her students. The classroom window was open, and Dr. Klee and I heard every word. After the teacher was through with her verbal assault, there was a long silence from Dr. Klee. She then looked me right in the eyes and said, "Ken, if we could only learn to put that much energy into our teaching, we would not have so many discipline problems." Her words echoed in my heart and are still echoing today.

I have not stopped ranting and raving since. The only difference is I rant and rave about what I'm teaching or the book I'm reading. It can be pretty scary sometimes to walk past my classroom. People often wonder what in the world is going on in there.

I can't expect my students to get excited about learning if I'm not excited about what I'm teaching. My passion for teaching manifests itself in my enthusiasm. If I lack passion, my students will be indifferent, as well. So get loud! Get excited!

60

Train Your Students to Focus on the Instruction

I teach my students to always make eye contact with anyone who is speaking to them. It does not matter who is doing the speaking. My students are required to listen to one another and any instructor with their eyes and body. I always use the illustration of someone going to a movie theater and facing away from the screen. Hello!

In addition to teaching my students to focus on the instruction, I also train them to not let external distractions interrupt their learning. When someone knocks on the classroom door, for instance, my students know to keep focusing on what we are doing and me. I teach them that the task at hand is more important than the distraction at the door, and that they are more important than any distraction and interruption.

This includes interruptions from other students and teachers as well. I was once opening presents from my students during our Christmas party when another teacher came to my door and asked to speak with me. I explained that I was busy with my students and that I would speak with her later. The teacher replied by saying that it was very important that she speak to me immediately. I simply looked at her and answered quite firmly that what I was doing with my students was also very important. I then returned my full attention to my students and the gift opening.

I always choose to put children first. Unless it's the principal or another administrator, I answer the door and respond to interruptions on my terms, when I am ready. I have a reputation for being very difficult in this area, but I offer no apologies, and I have no plans to change.

61

Be Positive

I have a sign at the entrance to my classroom that reads "No Negative Thoughts Beyond This Point." It is a reminder to students, parents, and me. I always try to look on the positive side of things. When I grade papers, I use checkmarks for problems that are correct, but I avoid using Xs to mark incorrect answers. I also try to use green ink when grading rather than the traditional red because red ink can have such negative connotations.

When it is time for seatwork practice, I tell my students that I will be circulating throughout the room trying to catch somebody doing the *right* thing. When you have a positive outlook, so will your students.

62

Teach Your Students Not to Whine

I don't do very well with whining from students or adults, so right up front I let my students know that whining will not be accepted. My students know that I expect them to work hard, have self-discipline, and complete homework without whining. Once they learn that whining will not be tolerated, it magically disappears. Whining has to be confronted and eradicated as soon as it happens because it can be quite contagious.

63

Sing with Your Students

Singing is a great way to teach reading. There is rich language in music. A piece like Harry Chapin's "Cat's in the Cradle" is great to start off with if you have never integrated language arts and music.

When studying a song with my students, I introduce its words first. We read the piece and discuss it based solely on its literary content. Afterward, I let the students know that the words they just read are actually from a song. I then play and sing the song for the students and get them to join in as they become more familiar with the tune.

You can always sing along with a tape or CD if you don't happen to play a musical instrument. I find that my students love to sing. Christopher Cross's "Sailing" is another one of my favorite classroom songs. I use it with the Chris Van Allsburg children's story *The Wreck of the Zephyr.* I also love to use the Bill Nye science series because the end of each episode incorporates music dealing directly with the science topic covered.

64

Cook with Your Students

There are several opportunities throughout the year to incorporate cooking into the curriculum. Cooking is not only a fun enrichment or extension activity, it also allows students to practice reading recipes and following directions.

Literature lends itself nicely to cooking in the classroom. One of my favorite cooking activities is pizza, which we traditionally do after reading Jerry Spinelli's *Maniac Magee*. Maniac Magee, the main character in this book, happens to be allergic to pizza!

Who can resist a plate of tasty pancakes after reading *Miracles on Maple Hill* by Virginia Sorensen? A study of Native Americans or westward expansion in social studies offers great opportunities for cooking fry bread, a tasty treat.

Students love to put on aprons and take the role of real-life chefs when we engage in our cooking projects. Mrs. Drake, our cafeteria manager, always supports me in my cooking projects by assisting us in any way she can.

65

Use Theme Days to Make Every Day Special

I learned this strategy way back in the '80s, and I still use it today. It involves having special themes for a few days each year. I typically run theme-day sessions for a week, or a few weeks at the most, usually in the spring. Themes I have used in the past include sunglasses day, poetry day, nature walk day, pet day, garden day, inside-out day, hat day, and blues day. Use your creativity to come up with themes that will interest your students. I always give my students the chance to suggest themes as well.

Another idea for theme days is to focus on one subject all day. I have held Science All Day (SAD) themes as well as Read All Day (RAD) and Math All Day (MAD) themes. Our math specialist, Judy Stubbs, initiated a school-wide Math All Day theme which has our whole school take part in fun and exciting math activities.

66

Change Routines and Mix Things Up

Although getting into a routine is something I strive for, I occasionally find it necessary to mix things up a little. This keeps the school days from becoming stagnant. Changing the routine can mean simply switching the times for math and reading or going out for break at a different time for a few days. It can mean an extended reading day or no homework for the night.

67

Work Your Students Hard

I work my students hard, even on the very first day of school. We use the swimming pool analogy. If the water is slightly cold in a swimming pool, you're better off jumping in and getting it over with rather than slowly inching your way into the pool. We start hard right off the bat, usually touching on every subject area on the first day. I give homework on the first day as well. This sets the tone for the school year for my students. They know that even though we will have a lot of fun over the year, I will demand a lot of effort from them.

One of my former students, Paul Moon, was asked what he remembered most about his fifth-grade year with me, and he responded that he had the most fun he'd ever had, but that he also worked harder than he had ever worked before. I am a firm believer in working hard, and I expect my students to do the same. I tell my students that I can't do my job as a teacher if they don't do their job as students.

At the end of the day, it should be our students going home needing a nap, not us.

68

Know When to Relax

Just as important as working hard is knowing when to relax and back off. All work and no play is not healthy. My students and I need days to recover and regroup. There's no set timetable for this; it just depends on the particular students I have and how intense our studies have been.

69

There's a Time for Everything

My room has often been described as organized chaos. I am quite fond of variety, but in order for my class to have structure, I have to teach my students that there is a time for everything.

My students are trained to move from high-energy activities such as creative dance raps to more tranquil activities like silent reading in a matter of minutes so we don't lose instructional time. I let them know that in order to do fun, exciting activities, we have to be masters of transitions.

Most teachers shy away from activities that are fun and exciting because they are afraid of losing control of the class. This takes practice, and modeling is a vital part of the training process. There is a time to get loud and crazy and a time to be calm and tranquil. It is important to remember, however, that even high-energy activities should be done in an orderly way. To use an oxymoron we created a few years ago, students have to know how to *boogie gently*.

70

Engage in Brain Gym

I am very interested in the latest research on the brain and how students learn. This research shows that shorter instructional time periods followed by brief breaks allow the brain to rest and process learned information. We incorporate brain gym in the form of line dancing. We do a dance routine that involves the cross crawl and other brain-boosting steps. My students love the music and the dancing. The routine takes about five minutes, and then we get back to work.

As I began to learn more about the brain, I was pleased to find out that a lot of the activities I had engaged my students in for years are brain based. This just validated what I already knew was good teaching. There are a plethora of books available on the brain, movement, and learning. Give some of the activities they describe a try, and I think you will be pleased with the results.

71

Mozart for the Mind

I had been playing classical music in my classroom long before I heard about the research on Mozart. My students learn to enjoy classical music because I play it all day long as background music. Parents have praised me for introducing their child to classical music. The only time I don't have classical or soft jazz playing is when I am reading to my students.

The appropriate music creates a pleasant, tranquil atmosphere in the classroom that is conducive to learning. Our brain gym music is lively and upbeat, and I also use music when we move from one subject to another. I simply tell the students that I would like them to be ready for the next activity by the time the song is over. This eases the transition from one activity to another, and it also allows them to sing. I use a variety of music for transitions.

72

It's Intelligent to Ask Questions

As teachers we have to create an atmosphere that makes our students feel comfortable asking questions. If students know that they will be laughed at and ridiculed, they will never seek help. I have a large sign hanging on the wall of my classroom that reads *"It's Intelligent to Ask Questions."*

Although students often ask questions in front of the whole class, I handle most questions one-on-one and in small groups when I am circulating around the room. This is another reason I move about the classroom as I teach.

73

Take Control of the Class

Take control of your class on the first day of school—and never relinquish it. This is probably one of the best pieces of advice I can give to a teacher, new or experienced. No, I am not a dictator, but my students have no doubt who is in charge of the class. I take control the very first day, and I never give it up. My students want boundaries, and I gladly set them.

Students like classes where learning takes place in an organized way. I gain my students' respect when they know they will be learning in an environment where the teacher is in control or "with it" (understands what is going on in the class). I emphasize the team concept, and I am on my students' side, but they know that I am the coach and they are the players.

One way you can let your students know that you are in control is to handle all minor discipline problems yourself. Some teachers send students to the office or involve an administrator for every little thing, which causes them to lose their authority as the class leader. As best as you can, try to handle things in-house. Yes, there are occasions that warrant the immediate attention of an administrator, but don't bother with this for the little stuff. You may not only lose the respect of your students, you may cause your administrators to wonder about your ability to manage your class.

74

Discipline Quickly and with Dignity

Discipline is not synonymous with punishment. In order for your students to respect you, you have to respect them, and discipline with dignity. Dr. Paul Phillips, a wonderful psychology professor I had in college, taught me to discipline quickly, firmly, and quietly. This works very well for me. I don't dwell on a student's behavior, but address it and get immediately back to teaching.

Not all behavior can be handled quietly and one-on-one. At times I have to confront a situation firmly and in front of the other students. I still do this quickly, with an immediate return to learning.

I believe that once your students know that you care about them, they will allow you to discipline them. Yes, students choose whether they will submit to discipline or not—once they know that discipline is for the good of the class, and it is their behavior that needs to change, they learn to receive corrective words and actions in a respectful manner.

Dr. James Dobson's book *Dare to Discipline* also is a must read for any educator. It helped to shape my philosophy greatly in this area.

Work your students hard each day. This will keep behavior problems down because your students will be too busy to get into trouble. You can also try assigning challenging students a daily job or task that helps you out in some way.

Try your best not to get into power struggles with your students. If you ever find yourself battling with a student in front of your entire class, you had better win, decisively.

75

Encourage Perfect Attendance

I tell my students that if they are not at school each day, I cannot teach them all they need to know. I make them aware that our class is not the same when they are absent. One way I encourage perfect attendance is by having perfect attendance myself. I also reward students with a perfect-attendance candlelight lunch and an attendance medal at the end of the year. Having a fun, creative, and exciting class can do wonders for attendance as well.

In my twenty years of teaching, I have had only one student make it through his entire school career without missing a single day. Paul Moon arrived in my fifth-grade room with a perfect school attendance record. His goal was to go his entire school career without missing any days. Seven years later I attended Paul's high school graduation, where he was recognized for missing not one day of school his entire school career. Wow!

76

Post the Goals for Each Day

My students like to know what we will be doing each day. I used to tell them to wait and see when they asked what we would be covering for the day, but after doing a little more research into how students learn, I began posting daily goals on the blackboard each morning. Now my students know our goals for the day as soon as they walk into the room. This keeps me on target too. I usually check things off after they have been accomplished.

Recently my school implemented the practice of having teachers post essential questions related to the learning objectives for a particular lesson or unit. This helps to guide both student and teacher and helps teachers to focus their instruction.

77

Do Community Service Projects

Each year I engage my students in at least one community service project. This teaches my students to be involved in the community and gives them an opportunity to serve and help others.

As a class, we grow a vegetable garden each fall and donate our produce to the local homeless shelter near our school. Our garden usually consists of cabbages, collard greens, spinach, beets, and broccoli. This project incorporates math as well as science because the students must put into use what they've learned about area, perimeter, and measurement. My students also have the chance to use a garden tiller to cultivate the soil, a first-time activity for all of them. When the garden project is complete, we harvest the vegetables and take them directly to the shelter. The shelter is always appreciative of the fresh vegetables, and my students learn firsthand what it means to be a vital part of the community.

78

The Brightest and Most Wonderful

Two years ago the life of a former student of mine was abruptly cut short. Michael Btembke was clearly gifted with words. In fifth grade I introduced him to the wonderful world of poetry, and he quickly found out that this world was his home. After Michael died, I shared one of his poems with my colleagues. Eve Hunter, a dear friend of mine for my entire teaching career, who also knew Michael, sent me an e-mail stating that I had made Michael feel he was the brightest and most wonderful student in the world.

Her words thundered in my heart. Yes, that is my desire and goal for all my students. I yearn for each student to feel as though he or she is the brightest and most wonderful student in the world.

79

Show Yourself Friendly

I love to hear my students tell me that I am so nice, but I don't confuse being nice with being weak. Being nice and kind is a sign of strength, not weakness. Only strong teachers feel comfortable being nice and kind because they are not worried about their students getting the wrong message and taking advantage of their kindness. I am meek and mild, firm and strict, nice and kind.

A word of caution about being a friend: don't cross the teacher-student line. I am not my students' peer or buddy, but I am their friend. At times I have to teach my students this important difference.

When I am nice to my students, they in turn are nice to one another. One of the greatest displays of kindness I ever saw from a student came during our end-of-grading-period vocabulary bee. When the bee was over, a precious little girl named Anabel Ramirez approached me to ask if she could give the vocabulary queen a treat she had in her book bag. What a kind gesture on her part! A few minutes later, one of Anabel's close friends mentioned to me that Anabel did not get to participate in the vocabulary bee because I had failed to call her name. I had mistakenly left Anabel out of the bee. My heart was broken when I realized the error I had made.

We all learned a valuable lesson in kindness from Anabel that day. She didn't get upset at me; she didn't even tell me that I had forgotten to call her name and give her the chance to be vocabulary queen. She had prepared for the bee like the others. Her only desire was to personally present the winner with a treat from her book bag. I awarded Anabel Ramirez with the Principal's Award at our fifth-grade graduation because she epitomizes what it really means to be a team player.

80

Stay Physically Fit

The better physical shape I'm in, the more energy I can put into teaching. I keep fit by running. My life seems to make sense when I'm out on the jogging trail. I've also come up with a lot of creative and original ideas while running.

Teaching can be very stressful. You will end up being a desk teacher if you are not in good physical shape. Try to exercise at least three to four times each week. Whether you go to the gym, play tennis, or walk, do something physical so you can better meet the demands of teaching.

81

Use "Wait Time" When Asking Questions

I teach my students the difference between *reflective* and *reactive* thinking. The "wait time" technique gives my students the chance to engage in reflective thinking—it means letting them have time to think about what they are going to say before they answer a question. If I don't give them this time, but immediately call on someone else when they offer no immediate response (reactive thinking), they will have a harder time learning to verbalize their thinking and develop higher-order processing skills. Once my students know that I am going to wait till I get some sort of response, they become better listeners and thinkers. I do, however, allow my students to respond by saying, "I am not positive about the answer, but I think…" or "I am not sure about the answer."

82

Learning Styles

I sometimes give my students a learning style inventory at the beginning of the year. Lately, maybe because computer technology is a daily part of life now, it appears that most of my students learn best visually. I've changed my teaching style to adapt with this. Research is showing that we have to use graphic organizers and concept maps if we want students to remember what we are teaching them.

We have to move beyond our old ways of teaching if they are not proving productive. We old dogs have to learn new tricks and remain teachable.

83

Students Will Rise to the Level of Expectations

When students enter my class, they quickly find out what I expect of them and where I set the boundaries. They then respond accordingly. I have seen this happen firsthand in the lives of countless students academically and behaviorally.

I set high expectations and motivate my students to rise up to meet them. I look for excellence on a daily basis. This is easier said than done, but I stand firm and expect my students to perform at a high level. Excellence is not an accident. I expect the best from all my students, and I will not settle for anything less, no matter their background, race, or economic status. Students will rise to the level of expectations!

84

It's OK to Talk

A very popular comedian once said that school is the only place kids go to learn how to communicate where all they are told to do is "stop talking." I let my students know that in my class it is OK to talk. I base this on the concept that learning has to be social before it can be cognitive.

No, my students are not allowed to talk whenever they want. When I am talking or another student is talking, they must be quiet. My job is to provide ample opportunities throughout the day for my students to talk to one another in a structured format. Small group work and working with learning partners accomplish this. I want my students doing most of the talking, not me. Talk! Talk! Talk!

85

Choice Is a Powerful Motivator

One of the greatest motivators for getting students to produce is giving them a choice. When students are able to choose between even just two activities, they become empowered and motivated to work harder.

Having choices in life is a theme I refer to throughout the school year. I encourage my students to work hard in school and get a good education so that when they become adults, they will have many options open to them. Students who are not prepared and educated usually have to settle for what comes their way, but prepared students are able to choose the road in life they wish to take.

86

Remember to Compliment Your Students

I compliment my students frequently, not just on their schoolwork and behavior, but also on everyday things. I try to never let a student enter my room without noticing his or her new shoes, new hairstyle, new clothing, and so forth. The great thing about this is my students learn to do the same with one another and with me. They always have something nice to say when they see me wearing a neat tie or new shoes. In order to be good at this, you have to be what Polynesia the parrot instructed young Stubbins to be in *The Voyages of Doctor Dolittle*. You have to be a good *noticer*.

87

Always Celebrate Good Thinking

I teach my students to celebrate with clapping and praise when one of their classmates is successful. I let my students know that it doesn't take away from them when they recognize something positive about a classmate. I want them to be happy for a classmate who correctly answers a question they had also raised their hand to answer.

I believe strongly in competition, but I believe just as strongly in cooperation and support. I want to create an atmosphere where students get excited when someone has the right answer or exhibits creative thinking and problem solving. I know I am on the right track when students initiate the praise and applause and I join in.

88

Show an Interest in What Interests Your Students

When I show an interest in what my students are interested in, it's easier to get them to pay attention to the things that interest me, mainly whatever subject I'm teaching at the time. I try to know which musical artists my students listen to, which movies they watch and video games they play, and what their favorite television shows are.

Just because I'm familiar with my students' interests doesn't mean I condone everything they're into. There are a lot of musical groups, movies, and television shows that totally turn me off. I just find it helpful to know as much about my students as possible.

Although I am not a huge wrestling fan, I make it a point to know the names of the popular wrestlers, so I can communicate with my boys who are wrestling fanatics. This is what my students call being "with it," or being "tight," to use the latest slang. Being with it goes a long way in getting my students to produce for me.

89

Learn a Little Slang

I have found that keeping up-to-date on the latest slang helps me identify with my students. It also brings me immediate acceptance and makes my students more receptive to learning Standard English.

I have to be careful not to say something that is no longer "hip" (I mean "tight"), or I will hear it from my students. I am always careful not to go too far and cross the line between teacher and student, but I do enjoy having fun with the language in English and Spanish.

90

Celebrate Diversity

It is important to see diversity as something positive rather than negative. Norcross Elementary has several school-wide programs that embrace and celebrate diversity. In my classroom, we always make it a point to celebrate the different cultures of our students. Cinco de Mayo and Chinese New Year are yearly regulars for us. Students learn to feel proud of their culture and background when they are recognized and valued. We are, as Walt Whitman stated, "a nation of nations."

In Their Own Words

You can hear nothing better from your students than that something you said or
did had a positive influence on them.

Hey, Mr. A. It's Kim Spurrier, the funny redhead. I hope you still work at Norcross so you'll get this. I can't believe I'm already in high school! It seems like just yesterday we were performing the Punctuation Rap. I guess it seems like that 'cause the year I was in your class is still my favorite year, and you are still my favorite teacher!
Kim Spurrier

◆   ◆   ◆

Dear Mr. A,
I think you're a really nice teacher. You make me really smart and that's good because you've got to be smart in life if you want to be successful. I'm looking forward to a great year because you're my teacher, and I know you'll make me smart because you're good at it.
Your student,
Tiffany Mabe

◆   ◆   ◆

Dear Mr. A,
I really miss you a lot. Sixth grade is very boring. How are things going? I miss you, all the plays we did, all the fun field trips, and the night you, Erika, and I went to Cici's Pizza. (We didn't eat ten slices of pizza!) You don't know how much I want to do those things again. Did Cameron show you my grades and CRCT scores? I hope I made you proud. Miss you lots. See you at Lupita's.
Love,
Erin Abraham

◆   ◆   ◆

Mr. A, I will miss you a lot, and I will visit and/or call you. Thank you for everything. Thank you for teaching me people skills, being a gentleman, and being nice to one another. Thank you for taking me to a Braves game. I had lots of fun. Thank you again for everything. I want to say thank you by inviting you and a guest to see the Braves with my dad and me on June 11. It's a small way of saying THANK YOU!!!, but I know that you like baseball, and I hope to someday play in the Big Leagues. Mr. A, you are the BEST!!! I hope you have a great summer.
Antonio Callaway

◆   ◆   ◆

Mr. A, thank you so much for everything! So many of the skills you taught me in fifth grade have helped me succeed throughout the years. I appreciate the gift greatly, and I thank you for coming to my graduation.
Amit Momaya, salutatorian, Norcross High School, 2003

◆   ◆   ◆

Ode to Mr. Almon

Mr. Almon, you're the best.
You are the teacher above the rest.
Having you was lots of fun.
When we played baseball you always scored a run.
You helped your students be the best we could be.
I think the one you helped most was me.
I wanted to tell you it was lots of fun.
Mr. Almon, you are number one!
—Aaron Bradford

◆   ◆   ◆

Mr. A, It was so great to see you again after all of these years. I can still remember the wonderful times I had in your class, raising the flag every day, caring for the hermit crab, building my Quonset hut, and winning a trip to see them set up the teepee and Indian dancing. I can remember performing in the class plays and learning Spanish. Stay the awesome teacher you are! I mean, who else takes their whole class to Lupita's Mexican Restaurant so they can order their meals in Spanish? It was truly the best experience at NES being in your fun-filled class!
Thanks for the great times and stay in touch,
Thomas Lloyd II
PS Thanks again for being at my Eagle Scout Ceremony

◆   ◆   ◆

Hey, Mr. A,
Thank you for being there at graduation. You've always been the most giving person, and I appreciate everything you have done for me. If ever I can help, just let me know.
Alan Michaels

◆   ◆   ◆

Dear Mr. A,
I have a whole lot of stuff to tell you, but first I wanted to tell that I am really thankful to God because he gave me a chance to meet you and know you. He gave me a gift in you as another person to love me. I think sometimes that I am really lucky to have you as one of my favorite people.

Thank you for caring about me and not letting me down. During my hard times, I was thinking of you. I am glad for having a great, super teacher like you. Gracias.
Love,
Blanca Rivera

◆   ◆   ◆

Dear Mr. A,
Even though I couldn't attend your Birthday Bash, I just wanted to let you know that I love you and I love your teaching because you make learning fun. You're my FAVORITE teacher ever, and no one will ever replace you. I'm sorry that I couldn't go to your birthday party at Lupita's, but I still love you and I love the way you teach.
Your student,
Devin Summer "Big Papa Pump!"

◆　　◆　　◆

Dear Mr. A,
This is Anna Valdez (Dinah's twin), and I'm writing to you because it's teacher appreciation week, and you were my favorite teacher. Well, I'd like to thank you for being nice to me and Dinah when you read to us in Spanish, even though you didn't know us very well. Now that I'm in high school, I still believe you were my favorite teacher, because you helped me when I didn't understand English. You've helped me a lot even though you may not know it, and now I know how to read in Spanish. Part of that, Dinah and I owe to you. Well I hope to get to see you personally someday to say thanks. I wrote to say thank you, and tell you you've been my favorite teacher since kindergarten.
Sincerely,
Anna Valdez (kindergarten buddy class)

◆　　◆　　◆

Dear Mr. A,
What's up? I've been doing great at MHS. My language arts teacher told the class to write to our favorite teacher. Also the one who inspired you to move on to higher education. Well of course your name popped up in my head. Yeah, you've always been the tightest teacher and also the most inspiring to me.
Denny Dang

◆　　◆　　◆

Mr. A,
I remember it like it was yesterday. It was the year 2002, and I was in fifth grade. I had the best teacher in the world. You taught me never to give up and to believe in myself. If it weren't for you I probably would be cursing and doing bad things, but you taught me manners and responsibility. You are the best teacher ever.
Alex Hernandez

◆   ◆   ◆

Hey, Mr. Almon!
This is Marisol Membribes. I hope you still remember me. I was in your class in 1995. I was thinking about all the schools I've been to and decided to see if I could find your e-mail. I'm in college now, majoring in nursing. I've had many teachers, but you are still my favorite one. I hope you are doing well, and I hope my e-mail brightened your day!
Marisol

◆   ◆   ◆

Dear Mr. A,
Sorry I missed your birthday, but I'm all the way in Henry County. But I really miss you and your ways of teaching. Just wanted to tell you happy b-day. Still got it! Still got it!
PS Tell your new class I said hi! And everybody else!
Love always,
Alonte Jamison

◆   ◆   ◆

Dear Mr. A,
You have been a great teacher and a friend. WAR Day was great. The whole year was great. You have made my life brighter. You kept me smiling and laughing when nobody else could. I will never forget you as my fifth grade teacher and my friend.
Love,
Merical Jefferson

◆   ◆   ◆

Dear Mr. A,
I am writing this letter to thank you for coming to all my practices and games.
Thank you for everything, Mr. A. You are the best teacher in the world.
Mark Little

◆   ◆   ◆

Mr. A,
Things are going pretty well. I'm actually starting my life a little early. I joined
the Navy and ship out in July. I'm also getting married on March 20 and having
a little girl June 11. Other than that, just going to school and working. So how's
teaching? Well, I have to go. I hope you will attend my wedding.
Justin Ivey

◆   ◆   ◆

Mr. A,
Happy birthday and thanks for being there when I needed you. You have been
the best teacher I have ever had. You have always been so nice to me. So again I
say happy birthday!!!
Janet R.

◆   ◆   ◆

Dear Mr. A,
Surprise!! It's me, Zully. I miss you so much. I hope you can write back. How
has your year been? I miss you so much sometimes I could cry! I suppose this is
because you are not just my teacher, you are my friend. I still love you and think
you're the best teacher ever. I love the way you taught math. I think you were
the best math teacher ever because you made it so exciting and fun. Right now
the memories are released and tears fill my eyes. They joys of my fifth grade year
are unforgettable and so real. I love you, Mr. A.
Sincerely,
Zully Conde

◆   ◆   ◆

Dear Mr. A,
Terrific! Fabulous! These adjectives describe your great gift to me. Thank you so much for the cool crazy straws and the neat stencils. I used the talk bubbles in this letter. I'm glad you could join us at my house for the Thanksgiving feast. I hope you enjoyed it.
P.S. Maybe you can come for Christmas. Then we might serve you breakfast!
Love,
Megan Metzger

◆   ◆   ◆

Dear Mr. Almon,
I would just like to take this opportunity to thank you for being such a positive influence in Michael's life. He thought the world of you and always rated you as his favorite teacher of all times. Many times I had to explain to him that he could not just come to the school to visit, as it may be disruptive. Regardless of what Michael did or where he went, he always made certain that everyone knew that Mr. Almon will always be his favorite.

I have enclosed copies of some pictures that I have had since your class did the Motown skit way back in 1996, when Michael did Little Richard. I included a more recent picture also just for you.

Ghakarhi Btembke
Michael Btembke's dad

◆   ◆   ◆

Dear Mr. A,
I just received your letter today. In Detroit, we are out of school now. We got out on June 13. You know why you couldn't reach me? It was because that was my dad's telephone number from his cell. We finally got a telephone. By the way Mr. A, I actually didn't call you collect, I called you on a telephone card. Hey, at least you won't have to pay for the call. I miss you so much! Would you come visit?
Love,
Chiquita (Alejandra Vera)

◆   ◆   ◆

Mr. Almon:
I wanted to send you a message and tell you hello. We think about you frequently. You are still #1 on the list of teachers for Alex who is now in eleventh grade. I hope all is well with you. Alex has given up all sports except baseball. He is doing very well in baseball. He made the varsity team last year as a sophomore and was a starter and top contributor for the team. This year we hope for a really good season. We would love to have you come out to watch him this spring. He is six feet tall now and really starting to look like a man. Your name came up in conversation last night, and I decided to drop you a note while it is on my mind. This weekend he is going to Vanderbilt University to attend a baseball showcase and look around the campus. Time sure flies!! I will try and update you again after the New Year. Have a wonderful holiday season.
Gail McMullen (Alex McMullen's mom)

◆   ◆   ◆

Mr. A,
This is Stephen Harris. I was surfing the Web and decided to check out if NES had a Web site, and lo and behold, yes. And so I decided to look up one of my favorite teachers, you. How are you? How is your class? I am doing well. I have about three weeks left until graduation from the University of Tennessee. Then it is track-and-field training through the summer, and hopefully it will take me to the Olympic games in Athens, Greece. I am healthy and enjoying life. I hope this e-mail finds you well. Please holler back and fill me in on the happenings in Norcross.
Your student still,
Stephen Harris

◆   ◆   ◆

Dear Mr. A,

How are you doing? It has been such a long time since I last saw you and talked to you. How have all your classes treated you? Lori and I just visited your class Web site, and I want to say CONGRATS on the chess tournaments. That is so awesome that your class made it into state regionals three years in a row. Well, Lori and I are planning to visit you at the end of the school year, and are won-

dering if that's OK with you. Lori and I both really miss you…A LOT!! You are after all our favorite teacher of all time. Also, if you have time, please respond.
Miss you Mr. A,
Giang-ha Sy (class of 2000)

◆   ◆   ◆

Dear Mr. A,
You are so intelligent! When you hug me I know that you are the best teacher. I will never forget that you taught us to never give up and keep working.
Kasandra Acosta

◆   ◆   ◆

Dear Mr. A,
These past months have been wonderful. You taught me manners, you showed me new things, and you always give me new things. I liked everything you did, and everything was fun that you did. You are "best" fifth-grade teacher. I am really going to miss u! I wish I didn't have to leave, and also that school wouldn't stop. I wish there were more days in school (only in this class.) I am going to come and practice chess, and I'm going to be there for your b-day! Well, take care!
Your little chess girl,
Katia Amaya

◆   ◆   ◆

Dear Mr. A,
You are the greatest teacher I ever had. I will miss you when I go to sixth grade. You taught me all the stuff I need to go to sixth grade. I hope you have a great vacation. Thank you for letting us play soccer outside almost every day. Also, thanks for the awards you gave us.
Your student,
Allen Bracewell

◆   ◆   ◆

Dear Mr. A,
You have been a great teacher. You are a very hardworking man. You really changed my life. You turned Cs into As and Bs. I appreciated how much you've taught me. There is a time for having fun and times when we have to work and work. I want to thank you for all you have done for me. Thanks.
Love,
Your Flaquita
(Arely Trejo)

◆   ◆   ◆

Dear Mr. A,
Thank you for teaching me manners and for teaching me every subject. You have helped me get As and Bs. You have inspired me. Every time I see you it's like I never want to leave you. You are not like any other teachers. You are different. You have helped me reach some of my goals. You are the nicest teacher I have ever had.
Anabel Ramirez

◆   ◆   ◆

Dear Mr. A,
Thank you for everything you have done for me. I am so lucky to have you as a teacher.
Giovanni Coto

◆   ◆   ◆

Dear Mr. A,
How are you? I hope you're doing well. I really miss you. I think about you every day. Thank you for all the gifts you gave me. That was really thoughtful of you. The dog is really cute, and the book is interesting. I hope I can see you someday. Please send me some pictures of the class and you. Happy Thanksgiving.
Love,
Sefali Patel (moved during fifth-grade year)

◆   ◆   ◆

Dear Mr. A,
You were the greatest teacher. I'll miss you when I go to middle school. I'll always remember how you taught us manners and to never give up. I'll never forget how you read to us. You were always nice. You are the best teacher in the world. Thanks for everything!
Your student,
Pooja Patel

♦   ♦   ♦

Dear Mr. A,
You taught me manners, working hard, and to always be on task. I appreciate all the things you taught me. Mr. A, you are like a role model to us.
Your student,
Nhan Xa

♦   ♦   ♦

Dear Mr. Almon,
I will never forget you. I can't believe I am going to leave you. I enjoyed being in your classroom. Thank you for everything. Thanks for the Skittles and the teddy bear you gave me when I broke my leg. Thanks for picking me to have the ERA Spirit Award. And the last one, thanks for being my teacher. I had fun being in your classroom. We did a lot of drama, and that was fun. I never had a teacher like you. You always know how we feel, so you let us do a lot of drama. You are very special to me. I will never forget you, and I love you with all my heart.
Love,
Jeanna Nawar

♦   ♦   ♦

Hello, Mr. A:
I know it has been many years and many classes, so it may take you a moment to remember me, but I am hoping you do because I sure remember you. I was in your class back in 1985. I know it seems like forever ago. I just wanted to send you an e-mail telling you what a great influence you had on me, and that the things that you taught me stay with me to this day. I also wanted to congratulate

you on the Teacher of the Year award. You really deserved it. You make teaching fun! I hope you are well.
Danielle Thiery

◆   ◆   ◆

Hi Mr. Almon,
I know I am the last person that you would expect an e-mail from, but I have a problem and I am hoping you can help. The problem is with my fifth-grade son. I cannot seem to get him motivated to do his schoolwork or homework. It seems kind of funny that I automatically thought of you to help me with this, 'cause you somehow were able to motivate me to do better...I remember how great you were with our class and hoped that you might have some suggestions that would help. On a lighter note, I hope that this e-mail finds you well. I want you to know what a difference you made in my life and the lives of a lot of kids. You are a wonderful teacher. I look forward to hearing from you.
Thank you for all you do,
Kim Parris (Warbington)

◆   ◆   ◆

Dear Mr. A,
Hi, it's me, Janet. Chess club is over and that's not good because I am going to miss our Thursdays when Anna and I stayed. You know the picture frame I gave you? We need to take a picture of you, Anna, and me. You are the best teacher ever. I know I said it a million times, but it's true. The school year is almost over and guess what? I'm not happy because you are a good, kind, and nice teacher. You know that since the first year I came to Norcross Elementary I wanted to be in your class and guess what? I am going to miss you and times when we had fun, like when we went to go see Harry Potter. That was fun, and I'm going to say thank you again.
Love,
Janet Rodriguez

◆   ◆   ◆

Mr. A,

I would like you to know how much I appreciate everything you do for me. I would also like to let you know that you are one of my best teachers and always will be. When I think about sixth grade, and when I think about leaving your class I start crying because I don't know if I will ever get a teacher as encouraging as you. I love it when you encourage me because I feel that someone will help me meet my goals. I will make you proud of me. I don't know if you know how much I LOVE YOU!!!!!

Love,

Paula Delgado

◆   ◆   ◆

I miss you Mr. A. I miss the good-morning warm hugs. I miss your good teaching, your jokes, the way you do things, the way you read to us each day, the way you made learning easier and fun, the way you encouraged us to learn, the great way you teach, the way you made me work hard in my spelling, writing, and most important of all reading. Thanks, Mr. A, for *all* the things you have done for me.

Love you,

Nancy Quezada

◆   ◆   ◆

Dear Mr. A & class,

Hola, Como estas? Yo estoy muy bien. This postcard is San Sebastian; it is in north Spain. It is cold here, about 32 degrees every day. The people in the city were out on their sailboat and little fishing boats, anyway. I can now speak Spanish and understand it too. Thank you, Mr. A, for teaching me I could do anything I wanted.

Smiles,

Wendi Holland (soon-to-be medical doctor)

◆   ◆   ◆

Dear Mr. Almon (aka Mr. A),
Wednesday, December 19, 2001, will be Kenny's last day at Norcross Elementary. I hope to be able to meet with you. Kenny has had nothing but good things to say about you. You have had such a positive influence on Kenny. He's never spoken so highly of a teacher as he does you. For that, we thank you! Kenny will be attending Hapeville Elementary for the remainder of the year. We will also be together as a family, which is more important than anything else. This really brings joy to our hearts and peace to our minds. Again, thank you for caring—thank you for being the person and instructor you are. We could use a whole lot more instructors like you!
Sincerely,
Cynthia King (Kenny King's mom)

◆   ◆   ◆

Mr. A,
When my teacher told the class about teacher appreciation week and how you write to your favorite teacher, you are the only one that popped into my mind. I am writing to say thank you for all of the effort you put into teaching and making learning fun and worthwhile. You are the single most teacher that actually seemed to love teaching. With your energy and love of your career, the time you took to make your students understand and grasp hold of the knowledge, and my hunger to learn, school was fun. The plays we performed taught others while we were learning ourselves. Ahh…the good ol' days. Now that I am in the eleventh grade, I have experienced so many learning techniques, but yours was and always will be my favorite. Keep doing what you love and what you're good at. Keep up the good work!
I love you,
Erika Harris

◆   ◆   ◆

Hi, my name is Christy Morrow (Sims when I was in Ms. Adams class). You may not remember me, but you had a big impact in my life when I went to school at Norcross. I was not even in your class. My best friend Amber Smith was though, and she would tell me every day all the stuff you guys would do in class. You may remember, back in 1987 I believe, the girl that CLOGGED in the talent show. Well, that was me. I wanted to *thank you*. Like I said, even though I was not in

your class, your teaching style touched me, and I could never forget you. I hope this little e-mail finds you in great health and of great spirit. And Amber says hi. We are still friends after all these years. She has two wonderful children now and owns her own hair salon business. I will be giving her your e-mail. I know how you guys love hearing from students from almost twenty years ago.
Christy

♦   ♦   ♦

Mr. A,
Thank you so much for your consideration of my brother Stephen and I as we take yet another step away from the innocence and simplicity of youth towards…well, towards a stage of life that is not as innocent and simple. I'll never forget the time our class was at lunch in the Norcross Elementary lunchroom, and I decided not to participate in something that was popular (but not exactly right). There was some "static" being thrown my way because of this. You happened to have been observing the situation from a distance, and you intervened at the critical moment to silence my ridiculers and to thank and encourage me. This is one of the many experiences I had under your expert tutelage and mentorship that has helped to form me into the young African American man that I am today. I guess I'll end with an understatement (and a slight grammatical aberration). Thank you so much for everything that you have done for my family and me.
I love you, Mr. A.
Jonathan Harris

♦   ♦   ♦

Mr. A, it's been a long time since we last had a chance to speak to one another. I just got off work, and I was trying to find out what was going on at the new Norcross High School. While online I noticed NES's Web link, and thought I'd see how things were going for you. Your Web page looks good. Things have come a long way since I was there. I don't know if I've talked to you since I changed my major about a year ago, but I should be teaching in another year or so. I was only a semester and a summer from getting my management degree, and I had a change of heart. I know it was a huge pay cut, but I've come a long way and learned that money isn't everything. I hope you know you were a great influence in my life. Teachers have a power over the influence of young children that even some parents don't have. I was lucky to have the

parents I did, but I was also very lucky to have at least one teacher like you too. I'm glad to see that you continue to make that difference. I wish I could make it back to speak to your class, because I would love to meet them. It'll take some planning though with school and working full time. I can't begin to explain how excited I am about being a P.E. teacher. As a matter of fact, I think that I want to teach elementary and work with an after-school program too. I hope your year is going well, and hopefully we could see each other or talk before long.
Still Grateful,
Paul Moon

◆   ◆   ◆

Ken,
Saying I am proud of you just doesn't seem to express how I honestly feel. Your commitment is so inspirational. You are an amazing teacher and friend to me. I have looked to you for guidance, support, and a tender shoulder, and you have never failed. Thank you! Your children are blessed to have a wonderful and loving teacher!!
Love,
Crystal Marshall (former Norcross colleague)

◆   ◆   ◆

Ken,
I am so very proud of you. During the time that I taught with you, your innovative style obviously always held your students' attention, as well as their love. You were always easy to work with. Of all things, I don't think I ever saw anyone who enjoyed teaching more than you. God bless! Keep up the good work.
Love,
Katherine Carlyle (1984–1985 mentor)

◆   ◆   ◆

Ken,

I just wanted to let you know that your inspirational speech today absolutely floored me! I was crying like a baby because you have the incredible ability to reach our hearts and minds and uncover those emotions that we always feel, but sometimes struggle to show to others around us. I feel very proud to be a colleague of yours, and you are definitely an inspiration to everyone who is lucky enough to know you. Thanks for reminding me why I entered the teaching profession.

God bless you.

Webb Vandiver (Norcross colleague)

◆   ◆   ◆

Dear Ken,

I am so proud of you and for you. What a great honor, and it could not have gone to a more deserving teacher. I have thought of you often and told many people about you when "great teachers" are the topic of conversation. May God bless you and continue to use you to touch the lives of many students.

Friend,

Audrey Stewart (former Norcross secretary)

◆   ◆   ◆

Ken,

You are one of the best…a true teacher who knows there are no shortcuts. Continue your passion always. You are an inspiration to so many…students and teachers like myself. May one day your story be told in *your* book.

Helen Morris (former Norcross colleague)

◆   ◆   ◆

Ken Almon is not only an exceptional educator, he is a sincere, compassionate, and most important and unique individual. From the moment I met him, I knew he would instill in the minds of his students the significance of respect, compassion for others, the importance of an education, and most of all the leadership skills needed, which would impact their lives. I will forever treasure his friendship and the gift of love he gave our students. Ken is one of those

amazing individuals that we all benefit from having known. Ken, always remember, "People may forget what you say, and may forget what you do, but forever remember how you make them feel."
Cindy Antrim (principal when I began teaching at Norcross in 1984)

◆   ◆   ◆

As principal of Norcross Elementary, I had the opportunity for four years to work with a young teacher named Ken Almon. With the approach of each new school year, I soon learned to be prepared for the impending calls from hopeful parents desperate to have their child placed in Ken's fifth-grade class. Students were drawn to Mr. Almon for a number of reasons. One of his most distinguishing attributes as a teacher was his ability to build a rapport with each of the individuals in his classroom. Ken Almon realized that in order for his students to achieve a high level of academic success, demonstrate the willingness to take risks in the classroom, and appreciate the process of learning, his mission must include establishing a relationship characterized by a sense of emotional and academic support. Because this relationship was based on mutual trust and respect, Mr. Almon's students worked hard for their teacher and quickly learned the value of working even harder for themselves. An indelible impression is left on the hearts of scores of children who have had the good fortune to have a fifth-grade teacher named "Mr. A"
Dr. Janet Verner Hall (former Norcross principal)

◆   ◆   ◆

Ken Almon is one of the most dedicated teachers with whom I have worked in my twenty-nine years in education. Children all love him, because they know he loves them. I have seen him turn around the lives of many children who came from troubled backgrounds and not much support from home. Ken could go into administration or any other area of education, but for all these years, he has chosen to stay in the classroom with fifth-grade students at Norcross Elementary.
Gary Yetter (former Norcross principal)

◆   ◆   ◆

Ken, you are awesome!!! Your presentation was the best thing that teachers could have heard to start their year on a positive note. Just imagine all the many stu-

dents who will benefit from their teachers having heard your words to treat them with respect and dignity, care and love. The students will appreciate you talking to their teachers on their behalf. Ken, you make me so proud to be an educator and to have worked with you at NES. You reflected so much about NES, your family, you as a teacher and an African-American male. Thank you for saying "yes" when called upon to share "why you teach" with others. So many will benefit from your words. Have a wonderful year, Ken!!! Stay in touch with me. Keep soaring and hold fast to your dreams…
Jean Walker (former Norcross principal)

◆　　　◆　　　◆

Ken,
I have really enjoyed working with you. Words cannot describe the admiration and respect I maintain for you as a professional and colleague. I only wish you could teach high school students. Your means of motivating students to learn is so needed at all levels.
Best Wishes
Angela Pringle (former Norcross principal)

◆　　　◆　　　◆

Mr. A is every student's dream. He truly understands the importance of the student-teacher relationship and how it affects student motivation. I would feel comfortable with him teaching any child I know. The kids love him, the parents love him, and we love him at Norcross Elementary. He is truly the right person to write a book with this title. Share your knowledge, Mr. A.
Dr. Lavern Watkins (current Norcross principal).

◆　　　◆　　　◆

This is the first minute I've had to once again thank you for the wonderful presentation to the Dyer staff on Friday morning. It truly had a great impact on those in the audience. I do not know of anyone else that has spoken to the staff that has received a standing ovation, and that even includes me after I told them every Friday would be a Spirit Day. I do appreciate the time you gave us, and the message from a fellow teacher did more than anything I could ever say to them. I

hope you had a good opening day and have a good year ahead. Say hello to all my Norcross friends.
Phil Epperson (former Norcross assistant principal)

◆　　◆　　◆

Ken,
Congratulations! I am so proud for you. What an honor! You certainly are deserving of this award. I was thrilled that you finally have gotten public recognition for years of dedication to students.
Sandra Levent (former Norcross assistant principal)

◆　　◆　　◆

Ken,
You really are a wonderful person. I hope one day I can make learning as much fun as you do and will be pleased if I can develop a relationship with my students like you have.
Lisa Alliston (student teacher)

◆　　◆　　◆

Mr. A,
I cannot begin to express what these past seven weeks have meant to me. I have grown in so many ways, both as a teacher and as a person. Thank you for opening your heart to me and welcoming me into "your world." I will miss you all very much and cannot imagine not coming back on Monday to start the week over again. You have been an amazing inspiration to me, and I know that when I grow up I want to be just like you!! Thank you from the bottom of my heart.
Nicole Freedmon (student teacher)

◆　　◆　　◆

Mr. Almon
I'd call you Ken, but that just wouldn't be right; it's always been Mr. Almon. I was just watching *The Matrix* again, nothing on and nothing going on, and remembered how Laurence Fishburne always reminded me of you. I figured that

was as good a time as any to write, far too overdue in fact, and that gave me something to do.

I'm assuming you remember me, but I don't want to be presumptuous so let's see, fifth grade was what, I graduated in '92 so 12 minus five is seven, 92 minus…was it '85? That sounds right. I was good friends with Paul…Paul McSomething, McNeal maybe. I guess we weren't great friends. I was in the same class as Marsay Simpson and Matt Wyrick; sorry, I think I misspelled both of those. Anyway, I was in your class around that same time. I hope that helps. I am sure that between, 30 times 20, six hundred faces passing your desk, it becomes difficult to place them all, and I wasn't the most outspoken kid of my day so if you can't place it just right, no big deal.

I just wanted to catch up, or rather thank you by catching up, for the impression you left. It has many folds, the impression, so I'll name a few. One, every MLK Day you come to mind. I can picture the classroom vividly and the old record player you had there. I remember watching the record spin around close to the back door of the classroom while we listened to his speech. This was before the day was a holiday, but I recall your deep passion for the day itself and how we all had a holiday of sorts within your class. Looking back, that was probably better than the kids have it nowadays sitting at home in front of the X Box having no clue what the day is about. Well, except for your class. I am sure they still get the same response out of you.

Something else was the zoo visit, how you paired us off in threes, is there a word for that, and took us all to the zoo over the summer. I think that was the glue that really made you stick in the old noggin. Then there was the, what was his name, the Amazing Whatshisname, with the turban (I don't know if that went over well in the past few years), and the reading contest. He made me proud of reading, something I can't get enough of now. And there were other countless little things that made you my favorite teacher, but you get the point.

As for me, my love of education faded through the school years and I stayed a mediocre student at best. I graduated, yes, but just so. I tried the college thing, but my heart still wasn't in it so I joined the Marines. There I excelled in Security Forces in Greece and in the infantry back home. I found out who I was, not the Marine in me but the adult. After the Marines I went to work in construction with David McLeroy, whom you might know of. I worked with him for a few years, too many probably, until it came time for me to decide if that was the path I wanted to take. It wasn't, so I bailed and, through the help of a friend, got a job at Manheim Auctions, a subsidiary of Cox Enterprises, as a computer hardware installer, where I traveled the nation for a few years all the while learning about computers in my spare time.

My knowledge of computers, ability to manage people, and my national contacts scored me a spot as a supervisor for a small group in our IT department. All along the way learning, because that was something of renewed value to me, and so I took it up as a hobby. The way I see it, I have the rest of my life to learn everything I can, so there's no real rush. I don't have a degree, but now I don't "need" one now. I hesitate on saying that because they are valuable, but the job I have and training I've been through warrant more credit on a resume than a diploma can in this type of work environment. It is now the knowledge itself that is power, not the proof thereof.

That takes me to where I am now, a happy person living his life. And I don't hesitate to say that you deserve partial credit. When I look back, there are few that stand out: my mom, my dad, my best friend, a girl I once knew, my senior drill instructor, a sergeant of mine in Crete, Greece, and you. You all had a profound effect on me in many ways. I just thought you should know.

One more thing, which you may or may not already know, is that of my daughter, Layla Patterson, who is in third grade right now at Norcross; she's in Ms. Schumann's class. I think her cousin might be in your class now or was last year, Jessica Scarbrough; her last name might be different, Maddox maybe, and her other cousin is the little girl with leukemia. Anyway, with any luck two years from now, or a rather a year and change, she will be in your class. When it gets closer I'll put in a formal request, but for now I can just hope that she is afforded the same opportunity I was at her age. Trust me when I say that I've, on more than one occasion, asked her to let you know I said hello, but she takes after the young me and is almost too shy to speak.

I'll wrap this up seeing as how it's my bedtime, but before I go let me say thank you again. Thank you. I'm sure I won't be the first person to say it, but you are a great teacher.

Thanks again,
Richard Patterson

◆   ◆   ◆

Mr. A

He is there at all times
There when you need a shoulder
To lean on
There when you need ears
There to speak to your heart
There when you want to increase
Your knowledge
He is there when you need support
Like on soccer games
Or family events
Whether it is four in the morning
Or one in the afternoon
He is there…
At all times
Yet you would think that
He is only a schoolteacher
But he's not
For me he is my
Uncle most of all
But also he is my teacher, mentor, guide
Role model, encourager
This human teacher
Has something that other teachers don't
He has the ability to be friends with his
Students
And sometimes he even has the
heart of a child
I can cry in front of him
And not be ashamed
He, as my uncle looks out for me
He, as my friend knows me in and out

And also has ears for me whenever I need them
I think that he is amazing too.
—Paula Delgado

◆   ◆   ◆

Mr. A, what's up? This is Michael Btembke, your favorite student of all time. So how's things been going for you? I have some free time right about now, so I wanted to just hold on to my word by keeping in touch with you. I feel sort of poetic now, so I'm going to write you a poem, that is, after I talk a little more.

Right now I'm trying to talk to somebody about me joining some sort of sports/athletics program here at North Gwinnett High School. I'm really feeling bad that I didn't get to play football this year for Norcross Blue Devils. I remember when you came to my games in middle school and cheered for Kendrick, Frankie, and me from the bleachers. I really appreciate you always being there to support me. I knew that wherever I was, you were never too far behind me cheering me on.

You've been a real inspiration in my life and my academics. You got me started writing poetry, and now I'm one of the best in the county, I think. You were always one for phrases, so here's one that I wrote. *You may be handed a gift, but you are given a charm and from that, you are what you are.* Here's another one! *If you believe that you do not have any problems, everything has become your problem.*

Well, I'm going to go ahead and write that poem 4 u, OK!

Whom to You, I Pray

Thanks to you for everything
And whom to you, I pray
For giving me the strength,
And the love you give today.
Thanks for the excitement
And the urge for different thrill
Thanks for showing me
Thou shall not steal and will not kill
Thank you for the blessing of a

Touching and gentle voice
I call out to my teacher
Mr. Almon, you're my choice
As friends we often played games,
Harmless but still a game
The older I got, the stronger we grew,
But still I saw a blame.
I carry a black bag over my shoulders,
Empty as it weighs me down
It's filled with darkness, filled with hate,
But GOD keeps me off ground.
I know as much as the next person,
As much, but then I see
That there are few, who choose to know nothing,
And they know nothing, but me.
Thank you Mr. Almon, you opened my eyes
And now I know
That there's one out there, no different from me,
And angel I suppose.
My fifth-grade year, you let me know,
The talent I possess
So I'm sending a prayer to you,
And to your class, may GOD BLESS.
To the #1 teacher in the world, Ken Almon
This was from the heart, hope u like.

What You've Done

I was lost when I came to you,
But you knew at a glance
That I would be unique,
Then you gave this kid a chance
I reminisce on days gone by

On plays we used to do
I look up to your every word
And hope to be like you
You helped me achieve my best,
And never accepted, "I'm not good"
You never accepted excuses
Whether you're rich or from the "hood"
You helped me stop the anger,
And you helped me stop the hating
And all you did was give me a poem
The name, *The Road Not Taken*
I can always come to you,
Whether I'm mad or feeling down
You placed that trust in me
And made a smile of a broken frown
The focus is on you
Thanks for helping me like a son
I thank you for what you continue to do
And what all you have done.

My Favorite Read-Aloud Books

Below you will find a list of some of the books I've especially enjoyed reading aloud to my students during my career. They are in no particular order, and the list is not exhaustive.

Tuck Everlasting by Natalie Babbitt
Letters from Rifka by Karen Hesse
Out of the Dust by Karen Hesse
The Dollhouse Murders by Betty Ren Wright
Wait Till Helen Comes by Mary Downing Hahn
A Time For Andrew by Mary Downing Hahn
The Best Christmas Pageant Ever by Barbara Robinson
Miracles on Maple Hill by Virginia Sorensen
Alexander and the Terrible, Horrible, No Good, Very Bad Day by Judith Viorst
Kensuke's Kingdom by Michael Morpurgo
Esperanza Rising by Pam Munoz Ryan
The Shiloh Trilogy by Phyllis Reynolds Naylor
Mrs. Frisby and the Rats of NIMH by Robert O'Brien
Where the Red Fern Grows by Wilson Rawls
Maniac Magee by Jerry Spinelli
J.T. by Jane Wagner
The Watsons Go to Birmingham—1963 by Christopher Paul Curtis
Nightjohn by Gary Paulsen
Skinnybones by Barbara Park
Sadako and the Thousand Paper Cranes by Eleanor Coerr
Bridge to Terabithia by Katherine Paterson

Closing

What an interesting journey it has been for me to share my philosophy, ideas, and strategies for teaching! The great educator Benjamin Mays has said, "The mind is and always will be our primary business." I love this quote. It says so much. Norcross students even have it on their chess club T-shirts. As educators, we should really accept it as our motto. The mind really should be our primary business. Once our students embrace this philosophy, the learning really accelerates. However, I don't believe we should focus only on academics. We also need to focus on the personal and social side of teaching. This will make the academic side easier, and students are more receptive to learning once they know they are cared for and accepted. Once our students believe in us, they'll follow us anywhere.

It's hard to believe that I have been teaching for twenty-one years. I have seen so many teachers come and go at Norcross Elementary, but I have chosen to stay. I am living proof that a teacher can remain in one place and still grow. It seems like only yesterday that I was trying to survive my first year with my thirty-five students. I still get nervous the night before the first day of school and teary-eyed on the last.

I have had so many proud moments as an educator, and I dare not try to list them all, but I have to recognize Kim Foster, Stephen Harris, Charity Cash, Quincy Crumbley, Crystal Sanders, and Paul Moon, all former students of mine, who have followed in my footsteps and are now making a difference in the lives of their own students. What a tribute!

About the Author

Originally from Tallapoosa, Georgia, **Ken Almon** has been a fifth-grade teacher at Norcross Elementary School in Gwinnett County, Georgia, since 1984. Almon has a bachelor's and master's degree in middle grades education from the University of West Georgia. He received the PTA Outstanding Educator Award in 1987, and he was awarded an honorary lifetime PTA membership in 1990. Almon was selected twice by his colleagues to represent Norcross Elementary as teacher of the year, first in 1989–1990 and again in 1995–1996. He was selected as educator of the year in 1998 by Hopewell Baptist Church. He and his class received a special invitation to the governor's mansion to have lunch with the governor of Georgia in 1998. Almon's name has appeared multiple times in *Who's Who Among America's Teachers.* He was nominated for this honor three times by former students: Wendi Holland in 1996, Marcela Arroyave in 2000, and Kyrie Lantz in 2004.

In 1998, Almon was selected by the Milken Family Foundation to receive the National Educator Award for the state of Georgia. He was presented with a key to the City of Norcross in 1998, by Mayor Lillian Webb of Norcross, Georgia.

Almon has several hobbies, including running marathons (he has completed four of them), reading, gardening, playing chess, speaking Spanish, and playing guitar and keyboard. His students affectionately know him as Mr. A.

Bibliography

Jensen, Eric. *Learning with the Body in Mind*. San Diego, California: The Brain Store, 2000.

_____. *Brain Compatible Strategies*. San Diego, California: The Brain Store, 2004.

Coming soon from Ken Almon, a look into the life of his first year in the classroom.

Chronicles of a First-Year Teacher

Monday, August 27, 1984

This was the first day of my teaching career. My prayer this morning was simple and to the point: Lord, teach me how to teach, and teach me what to teach.

I have one of the largest classes in the school—thirty-five students. GIVE ME A BREAK, MAN!

A little first- or second-grade student asked me for a bite of my lunch today. Later on during the day, his teacher and he were at my classroom door. It had somehow gotten back to his teacher that he had asked for a bite of my lunch. She made him apologize to me. I felt sorry for the little fella—I told her it was all right and not to worry. Speaking of lunch, there were only three tables for my class of thirty-five. Each table seats six! What a scene! I almost panicked myself.

I gave my discipline lecture today and taped it. I have not had a chance to listen to it yet. Overall, today was a pretty good day. Oh, yeah, a little girl slipped in the lunchroom, and I almost started laughing. I then remembered that I was a teacher, and I was to set an example. It sure was funny, however.

I have been told that I have the two worst-behaving students in the school in my room. I'll leave it at that.

To top off my day, I received a note from a sweet little girl named Amy Middleton. The note said, "For a man teacher, you're OK, Mr. Almon."

I think I will make it, even though I have been grading papers for over three hours now.

PS I have just finished watching a movie titled *To Sir With Love*, one of my favorites. I know this movie was sent from God for a purpose. I can definitely relate to Sydney Poitier and what he taught his students.

Tuesday, August 28, 1984

Boy, oh boy, was today ever a long day. My students limited themselves very well the first half of the day, but all heck broke loose toward the end of the day. I had to take some time off their recess. So far, I have been pretty consistent in following through on punishments. Teaching sure does require a lot of patience.

During math Lynn Babb broke me up laughing. I had called on him to give me a particular concept on syllabication, and he did it twice. When I called on another student for the same concept, she couldn't give it to me. Lynn then replied, "They just won't listen to me, will they?"

I ended the day with a little storytelling, sharing a favorite story of mine about the Kushmaker. They loved it!

When I arrived home, I was exhausted. I crashed!

Wednesday, August 29, 1984

Today was a pretty good day. While I was teaching science, Mr. Krall, a fourth-grade teacher, sent me a note one of his students had written that totally cracked me up. The note read, "Bronco Buster, load 'em up, round 'em up!"

Today was the first day of science, and I really enjoyed it. My students are having a pretty rough time with limiting themselves. It's like they have not ever heard of self-discipline.

Tomorrow I will give the first test of my teaching career—spelling. I pray that my students will do well.

Thursday, August 30, 1984

Most of the kids did well on the spelling test. I will have to re-teach some students, however.

While I was reading the Shel Silverstein poem "Paul Bunyan," I ran across the word "hell" a couple of times. Boy, was I surprised! From now on, I am pre-reading everything. The kids seem to enjoy the time when I read to them. I am reading *Superfudge* by Judy Blume. It's a great book. I crack up laughing each day I read from it. Peter, a character in the book, was about to urinate on a plant in today's reading.

I think I will have to press down on Mrs. Carlyle's class. We switch classes for science and social studies. They don't take me as their teacher, just a guest or substitute.

I finally got extra food from the lunchroom ladies today! Wow, was it good!

Friday, August 31, 1984

The big happening of the day was Mr. T (me). I had told my students that if they had a good first week, that my friend Mr. T (a character from a show called *The A-Team*) would visit on Friday. I dressed up as Mr. T in college and can do a pretty good impersonation.

I went from class to class dressed up like Mr. T. The kids really enjoyed it. I scared one little kid half to death in the hall. The whole school was on the lookout for Mr. T. One kid who couldn't make it to school because of a broken leg called the school secretary and asked what time Mr. T was coming. I had not told my principal and instructional lead teacher about it. Everybody was in a frenzy thinking the real Mr. T was on our school campus.

Mr. T ended what you might call an exciting, very exciting, first week of school. Mr. T and the Kushmaker story were my two big guns. WHAT AM I GOING TO DO NEXT?!

978-0-595-36480-0
0-595-36480-2

Lightning Source Inc.
LaVergne, TN USA
14 August 2009

154915LV00009B/1/A